Living with the Late John Rogerson

To Fran — Enjoy! Sherri Rogerson

~ A Memoir ~

by

Sherri Rogerson

© Copyright 2012 by Sherri Rogerson

All rights reserved. No part of this book may be reproduced, stored in a retrieval system or transmitted in any form or by any means without prior written permission of the publisher, except by a reviewer who may quote brief passages in reviews to be printed in a newspaper, magazine, journal, or on-line bookseller.

ISBN-13: 978-1479220533 / ISBN-10: 1479220531

To contact Sherri with comments (although compliments are preferred) write to her at:

E-mail: livingwiththelatejohnrogerson@gmail.com

Cover Photograph by Sherri Rogerson
Cover Design by John Rogerson
& their daughter Betsy Wolf

Praise for *Living with the Late John Rogerson*

"Perchance to dream before you wake, then read a book for humor's sake? To read, or not to read **Living with the Late John Rogerson**: that is the question. Forsooth, I must proclaim and sayeth, Yes, thou musteth, tis a hoot! Hasten and feast your eyes upon m'lady Sherri's memoir post-haste!"
—William Shakespeare. Seconded by Anne Hathaway

"Friends, *Villagers*, Countrymen! Lend me your ears, for I come to praise Sherri, for *most merry* is her recent memoir **Living with the Late John Rogerson.** Huzzah! Huzzah!"
—Mark Antony

"John! John! Wherefore art thou, John? Art thou late once moreth? Methinks thou art most fortunate I be not thy spouse! Getteth with the program, Buster!"
—Juliet

What light through yonder window breaks? 'Tis Juliet, reading **Living with the Late John Rogerson.** Indeed m'love, so hath I! If you tickle us, do we not laugh? By Heaven, we do! By Jove, our sides splitteth!
—Romeo

"It is a far, far better thing to read **Living with the Late John Rogerson** than never to read at all."
—Charles Dickens

"She does not let you down one bit.
Telling stories, all a hit!
From there to here, from here to there,
Funny stories everywhere!"
—Dr. Seuss

"Once upon a midnight dreary, I found a book along my path,
I read it through and then again; it made me smile; it made me laugh!
Living With the Late John Rogerson. Read it now—it's lots of fun!
—Edgar Allan Poe

"I'm late, I'm late, for a very important date.
No time to say "Hello", "Goodbye",
I'm late, I'm late, I'm late!

It's fate, it's fate. I know I'm always late.
Why can't I keep myself on time?
It's fate, I'm late, it's fate!"

—The White Rabbit,
A.K.A. The "Late" John Rogerson

❧ THIS BOOK IS DEDICATED TO ☙

Family and friends
who were always interested in my writing,
who offered encouragement and cheer,
who laughed at my stories,
and made my day with kind words of praise.
It meant more to me than you will ever know.

CONTENTS

Living With the Late John Rogerson 1
706 Suffern Road - 1974 4
Mr. Allen 12
Artichoke Spinach Casserole - 1975 20
Barney Cards 23
Gettysburg 32
What Space Between My Front Teeth? 40
Dentoscope 1978 45
706 Suffern Road - 1978 54
Keesler Air Force Base - 1978 57
Tillie the Twirler - 1979 60
Hurricane Frederic 66
♫ *"We're in the Money"* ♫ 71
♫ *"The Stars at Night, are Big and Bright* ♫ 74
♫ *"What Goes Up, Must Come Down"* ♫ 79
Six-Pack Flabs 82
San Antonio – 1981 86
Merry Olde England - 1983 89
Ham Anyone? 94
RAF Bicester – 1984 98
Windsor Great Park 101
Arachnophobia 109
Green Around the Gills 114
Real Estate Moguls 119
Howdy and Aloha! - 1990 - 1991 121

Sheppard Memories - 1990-1995 .... *131*
My Odyssey - October 1995 ✈ *133*
Life in Oregon *144*
The Ham Sandwich *150*
The Lake Oswego Adult Community Chorus *153*
Alaska or Bust! *157*
Mosquitoes *160*
September 11, 2001 - 9/11 .... *164*
♪ It's a "Schmall Vorld" After All! ♪ *168*
'Mr. Villages' Moves to The Villages *171*
Call The Fire Department!!! *173*
Golf *177*
What Happened To Yesterday? *180*
His Kind of Girl *186*

Acknowledgments ℘ *192*

Living With the Late John Rogerson

We all know what it means to be late, right? Not on time, not punctual, delayed, tardy and past due. Yup, all of those.

When it comes to being late, my husband John Rogerson is a Grand Master, a virtuoso. It is, in fact, his *modus operandi*. Going way back, I am pretty sure his habitual tardiness began before he was born. In fact, I would bet on it.

Although John was born in November of 1943, it wouldn't surprise me to learn that his actual due date was in June. When I think about it, it makes perfect sense. He was just not ready to make his appearance in June.

Despite the doctor's prediction, John was far too busy doing other things—*important* things—that demanded his attention. He was probably contemplating his navel and wondering if his umbilical cord was a jump rope. He had hands to study and fingers and toes to count to make sure they added up to 20.

Loving exercise, John undoubtedly practiced deep knee bends, elbow thrusts and push-ups for hours on end in his 'tummy' world. It was also the ideal time to practice dance steps to music only he could hear. No, that long trip down the ole' birth canal would just have to wait.

I have been married to John for over 46 years and getting him anywhere, *on time*, has been a major challenge in my life. No, make that a constant battle.

It wasn't a huge problem when we were first married. I would remind him when it was time to go somewhere, calling out that we had to leave in five minutes. He would reply "Okaaay" which was 'John-speak' for 10 minutes more as he jumped in the shower.

But over time that "Okaaay" stretched to fifteen minutes, then twenty. As I waited, expecting John at any moment, he was nowhere in sight. Where the heck *was* he and what was he doing?

Going room-to-room, I once found him in our bedroom crawling around on his hands and knees, searching for a pen he had lost ... a *week* earlier. Another time he was straightening up the bookcase in his study that had needed attention ... for months.

The corker was when he went into our bathroom to brush his teeth. When he didn't come out after twenty minutes, I opened the bathroom door and found him rearranging our medicine cabinet!

It's true. John is a bundle of energy and tries to keep a dozen projects going at once. The problem is that he never knows when it's time to call it quits and put his project 'on hold'.

Even when we are finally heading out the door, John discovers that he can't find his car keys, his wallet or his sunglasses. In other words, even when he says he is ready, John is never really completely ready. As the expression goes, John will probably be late to his own funeral ... and consequently, I may be early to mine!

We have lived in Florida for the past eleven years and John's reputation for being late is known far-and-wide. It is a given. He is involved in many, many activities—clubs, swim team, bands, choirs, benefit shows, musicals—and everybody knows he runs late. He skids into every meeting/rehearsal/practice with seconds to spare. If he has an 8 a.m. rehearsal and he gets there at 7:59 a.m., he thinks he's early!

I have come up with a plan. Just like Cape Canaveral, I am now a Mission Control Specialist. A half-hour before we are due to leave, I start my countdown. I march to the doorway of whatever room he is in and, in a loud voice, I announce:

> "WE ARE LEAVING IN 30 MINUTES.
> HAVE YOU CHANGED YOUR CLOTHES?
> ARE YOU READY TO GO?
> IF NOT, PLEASE GET READY."

Of course, I am already dressed and ready to go.

Ten minutes later, if I see he still has not stopped doing whatever it was he was doing ten minutes earlier, and believe me, he never has, I give notice again:

> "WE ARE LEAVING IN 20 MINUTES.
> HAVE YOU BRUSHED YOUR TEETH AND COMBED YOUR HAIR?
> DO YOU KNOW WHERE YOUR WALLET, YOUR KEYS AND YOUR GLASSES ARE?
> IF NOT, FIND THEM PLEASE AND GET READY."

Does this tactic work? Heck NO! And if anyone has any suggestions, I'd appreciate hearing from you! Honestly. Getting him out the door is like pulling teeth. And *he* was the dentist!

They say there's a fine line between 'reminding' and 'nagging'. I passed both a lifetime ago and have the white hair to prove it … what hair I have left that is!

The only reason we ever get *anywhere* ON TIME is because of me. I like being on time. I want to be on time. I am not only on time, I am usually early.

But if it is just John going somewhere by himself—*sans* me, and without my constant nagging/reminding/prompting countdown—forget it. He does NOT get there on time.

Consequently, everybody thinks I am a widow. All they hear about is the 'late' John Rogerson. ☺

☙❧

706 Suffern Road - 1974

Hello again and Welcome to my Sequel!

I hope you will find these stories entertaining and amusing. While they are all true, you will again appreciate why this writer went from being a brunette in her 30s to prematurely gray in her 40s, turning quite white in her 50s to Q-Tip white in her 60s, obviously waaay before her time. But I get ahead of myself ....

In my first book, *Don't Set The Alarm!*, I told the story of my life from 1944, the year I was born, to 1974, the year I turned 30. I am now 68-years-old and boy, have I got more stories to tell!

In the summer of 1974, an entirely new chapter in my life was about to begin. John and I had been married for almost eight years and we had already moved six times. Now there was the possibility that I was going to become the wife of a dentist! Whoa ... who'd a' thunk it?

With our young daughters Jennifer and Betsy and our Olde English sheepdog Barney, we were getting ready to move from Sun Prairie, Wisconsin, back to New Jersey. John was about to begin four years of dental school at Fairleigh Dickinson University in Teaneck—Move #7.

And to think, during the first twenty-two years of my life, I had not moved at all. Now I was averaging a move every fourteen months.

In addition to our Plymouth Valiant, we had needed a second, bigger car when we moved to Sun Prairie, so we'd bought a Dodge Sportsman Van that seated eight.

With each of us driving a vehicle, we "car-vanned" (Booo!) back to the Garden State, arriving in early August.

At first, we alternated living with our parents, driving the seventy-five miles between their homes. We then started looking for a home in Teaneck.

John and I had decided that the smart thing to do was to buy a house, hopefully not too far from the dental school. We were going to be in one place for four years. Why pay rent for forty-eight months and have nothing to show for it when it came time to move again?

As luck would have it, on the first day of our search, we saw a FOR SALE sign on the front lawn of a small two-story Dutch colonial at 706 Suffern Road in Teaneck.

Even though it only had a single-car garage, the best part was its location ... half a block from River Road. Fairleigh Dickinson University was on the other side of River Road and the dental school was a little farther across a footbridge spanning the Hackensack River. It could not have been more convenient. John would be able to walk to his classes!

John phoned the listed realtor and we crossed our fingers, hoping that the house would be in our price range—CHEAP! We didn't know what to expect, having never bought a home before. We didn't know that you could ask how long a house had been on the market or that you could make an offer. We thought that the price of a house was the price you paid. We're talking Babes-In-The-Woods here, folks.

The realtor called the homeowners and they said we could see their house right away. We learned that the house was owned by an older couple, the Fischers, who were moving to a retirement community in southern New Jersey.

The house had been built in the 1920s so it was already fifty years old. It had a handsome fieldstone façade and the walkway brought us up to the porch and front door.

As soon as we walked through the front door, we stepped into the living room. There was a stairwell off to our right that went up to the second floor. The living room blended into the dining room that had an in-the-window air conditioner the size of a VW Beetle. A small eat-in kitchen and an unheated, glass-enclosed back porch completed the first floor.

Stairs from the kitchen went down to a full basement. The back half of the basement was filled with what looked like a grain silo resting on its side. I learned that it was the home's fuel oil tank. Three bedrooms and the home's only bathroom were on the second floor.

We held our breath as we asked the realtor the price.

$46,000. **$46,000???** Gulp.

John had had to accept a demotion from captain back to 2nd lieutenant to receive Air Force sponsorship of his dental school education. His salary was going to be reduced by 25%, more than $4,000, since the Air Force was going to pay his tuition, books and fees, which came to around $14,000 a year. The reduction in rank and pay was understandable, but $46,000 for a house? Holy Schmoly! Make that 706 "Suffern' Succotash" Road!

All I can say is thank heavens John was in the military. We got a VA loan and did not have to put down a down payment. That made it possible for us to buy the house.

Due to all the necessary steps and reams of paperwork involved—bank verifications, inspections, appraisals and real estate rigmarole—we would not be able to close on the house and move in until the beginning of October. John's classes started in September shortly after Labor Day so we had a problem. We needed a place to live for at least a month.

The Fischers moved out of the house at the end of August. Even though we had not had the official closing, the Fischers were kind enough to give us a house key so that we could do some interior painting before we moved in. All the rooms in the house had been painted turquoise and I wanted something, uh … how can I say this … less turquoise.

Taking advantage of the long Labor Day weekend and for our eighth wedding anniversary, John and I gave each other gallons of primer and paint, paintbrushes and rollers, roller trays and drop cloths. Nothin' says lovin' like Sherwin-Williams.

Borrowing my parents' stepladder, we proceeded to paint the living and dining rooms a soft yellow and the woodwork and baseboards a semi-gloss white. This brightened both rooms considerably. Having now had enough fun for the holiday weekend, we decided to tackle other rooms and house projects after we moved in.

Dental school started a couple of days later so we did a flip-flop. John moved in with my parents in Closter, New Jersey, fifteen miles north of Teaneck. From there, he had a half-hour commute to the dental school.

My grandmother, Freda Hawthorne, still lived in her home at 110 Poplar Street in Ridgefield Park, only eight miles from our Teaneck home and one of her widowed sisters, Bertha Rice, a.k.a Aunt Bud, had moved in with her.

Meanwhile, Jennifer, Betsy, Barney and I moved in with John's parents in their home in Princeton, sixty miles south of Teaneck. I had been able to get Jennifer enrolled in kindergarten at an elementary school near their home on a temporary basis and John drove down to see us on weekends.

We closed on our Teaneck house on Monday, October 7th, with move-in on Tuesday, the next day. What an exciting, *thrilling* day it was going to be. I could hardly wait. We were going to be the proud owners of our *own home* for the *very first time*.

John had a full schedule of classes that Tuesday morning but I told him I would be fine. I assured him that I was perfectly capable of handling this move-in all by myself. After all, I was a *seasoned* Air Force wife with six moves under my belt and if there's one thing military wives know, we know moves.

Really, what more was there to do other than to tell the movers where each carton went, which piece of furniture went where, and to check off each item on our inventory sheets as the number was called out. It would be a breeze, a veritable 'piece-of-cake'.

The night before our move-in, Jennifer, 5, Betsy, 3, Barney and I stayed with John in my parents' home. John left for school early that Tuesday morning while the girls, Barney and I met the moving van in front of our Teaneck house just after 8 a.m.

While the moving van driver positioned the van in front of our house and his helpers opened various doors to begin offloading, I put the girls, their favorite toys and books, along with Barney and his water dish, on our empty back porch. I asked them to please stay there and to play quietly.

Remember that used brown and gold shag carpet that we had bought in Sun Prairie, Wisconsin and moved with us to New Jersey? To refresh your memory, it was the carpet with the imprint of a flattened mouse on its underside! (*Don't Set the Alarm!* page 185).

That shag carpet had been cut into two large pieces to cover the expansive living room and dining room in our military ranch house in Sun Prairie. A long matching runner ran down a hallway to the bedrooms.

Now in our Teaneck home, I wanted to put one of those large shag pieces in our living room, the other in our dining room. I wanted the runner to be used on the stairs going up to the second floor. The carpet would cover and protect the hardwood floors and look like wall-to-wall carpeting ... almost.

I asked the moving men to bring in the large pieces of shag carpet first, asking that they leave the long runner out on the driveway. John and I would deal with that another day.

Carrying in one long roll of carpet, two men dropped it on the dining room floor under the air-conditioner while the other carpet roll was dumped on the living room floor.

"Okay ma'am," the head mover said, "Please get the carpet in place as fast as you can so we can start bringing in your shipment."

Peeling off the packing tape, which held the carpet roll together, I unwound the living room section first. While it covered most of the floor, it was a job positioning it by myself, *turning* it around a few times, *pulling* it this way, *yanking* it that way.

In doing so, I realized that I had a problem I hadn't anticipated. I couldn't get the carpet to lie flat because of the large coiled radiators, each standing on four feet, along the walls of the living room. The feet prevented the carpet from reaching the baseboards and as a result, the carpet was all hilly and lumpy.

Oh great. Now what was I going to do? Somehow, I had to cut the carpet so that it would slip around those radiator feet. Did I have a knife? No! Did I have a pair of scissors? No!! Did I know a neighbor to borrow something to cut with? No!!!

I *jogged* out to our Dodge van where John kept a tool kit for road emergencies. While the movers smoked out by the moving van, waiting for me, I rummaged through the kit. There were no scissors or knife but I found several boxes of single-edge razor blades so I grabbed them.

Sprinting back into the living room, I dropped to my knees in front of the radiator nearest the front door. Pulling the carpet edge over onto my lap, I tried to estimate where it would hit the radiator feet. Grabbing a razor blade and squeezing it tightly between my thumb and index finger, I began to saw back and forth.

Saw!-Saw!-Saw! Cut!-Cut!-Cut! Saw!-Saw!-Saw! The carpet's burlap-matted bottom was old, dried out and tough, making it hard to cut.

Saw!-Saw!-Saw! Cut!-Cut!-Cut! Slice!-Slice!-Slice!

After I had made a four-inch slit, I pushed the carpet under the radiator as far as it would go. The carpet still would not lie flat; the slit wasn't long enough. Darn! I pulled the carpet back on my lap, grabbed the razor and sliced some more.

Cut!-Cut!-Cut! Slice!-Slice!-Slice! Saw!-Saw!-Saw! Slice!-Slice!-Slice! ... take a deep breath ... Cut!-Cut!-Cut! Slice!-Slice!-Slice! My arm ached, my hand cramped, and I was getting really hot.

Cut!-Cut!-Cut! Slice!-Slice!-Slice! Gads, this was impossible.

Finally, the slit was long enough and the carpet slid around the radiator's left feet to the baseboard. Now I had to do the same for the right side feet.

Cut!-Cut!-Cut! Slice!-Slice!-Slice! Cut!-Cut!-Cut! Saw!-Saw!-Saw! As perspiration beaded on my forehead and face, it ran down my neck and I started panting.

"**Hey Lady!**" one of the movers shouted from outside. "**Hurry it up! We don't have all day, y'know!**"

Cut!-Cut!-Slice!-Slice! ... **EeeoowwwOUCH!**

I dropped the razor blade and looked at my hand. A huge blister had popped open along the side of my index finger where the razor blade had rubbed against the skin. It burned and hurt like heck!

Running back out to our Dodge van where I'd locked my purse, I found a bandage that I kept in my wallet for emergencies. I wrapped it around the stinging blister but knew that it would come off quickly with the friction of the razor blade.

I *dashed* back into the house and flew upstairs to the bathroom. I ripped off several sheets of toilet paper and wound them around the bandage, hoping the padding would keep the bandage from coming off.

Racing back downstairs, I grabbed our seventeen-page inventory, resumed cutting slits in the carpet and yelled "**Okay**" to the movers outside. With that, they started carrying our goods into the house and began shouting out numbers for me to check off our inventory sheets.

Cut!-Cut!—

"Number 85. Where do you want this?"

I stopped cutting. It was our box spring. I flipped through the pages of our inventory looking for #85. "In the master bedroom." I said, pointing upstairs. I wiped my forehead with my left hand and checked #85 off the inventory sheet with my right hand.

Cut!-Cut!-Slice!-Slice!-Sli—

"Number 247. Where does this go?"

I flipped through the inventory pages looking for #247 and checked it off. "In the kitchen."

Part of the carpet was still bunched up in folds by the radiator. The movers proceeded to trip over it every now and swore under their breath.

"C'mon Lady! You're going to have to get this carpet flat or we won't be able to continue bringing your stuff in. It's too dangerous! Number 91 and 233. Where do you want these?"

Scrambling to find #91 and #233 to check them off, I replied, "Aaah ... #91 goes in the upstairs bathroom, #233 in the basement."

I moved to another radiator and kept slicing frantically while checking off inventory numbers, but cartons and furniture were coming into the house at breakneck speed.

The razor got dull so I grabbed another one. Trying to catch my breath, I saw that my protective wad of toilet paper was shredding and my right thumb and index finger were frozen in position. Perspiration was now running down my back

Suddenly an ear-splitting scream came from the back porch, followed by **"Mommy! Mommy!"** I jumped up from the floor thinking one of the girls had been seriously hurt. Jennifer came running into the living room with Betsy and Barney close behind.

"Betsy won't let me play with her Mrs. Beasley!" Jennifer wailed.

"Mrs. Beasley mine!" Betsy shouted, **"MINE!"** as she yanked Mrs. Beasley's blue dress and pulled her out of Jennifer's hands.

"MOMMY!" Jennifer shrieked.

"Oh for heaven's sakes!" I cried. "That's enough, girls! You are going to have to share. Betsy, you play with one of Jennifer's toys".

I led everyone out into the kitchen, gave Jennifer and Betsy a cookie and Barney a milk bone biscuit before returning them to the back porch. I reminded them that Mommy was very, very busy, they needed to play nicely, and to please share their toys. "And I don't want to hear any more arguing!"

Cut!-Cut!

"Number 206. Where does this...?"

Slice!-Slice!

"In the dining room."

"Number 34 ..."

Saw!

"Where"

Cut!

"Where do..."

The next thing I knew there was more screaming as the girls ran back into the living room. This time it was Betsy who was crying. **"Mommy, Jennifer hit me with her Snoopy!"**

"Number 119. Where do you want this?"

At that point, I didn't know whether to laugh, cry or just slit my wrists with the razor blade. Nah, that wouldn't have worked. It was too dull.

Around 11 a.m., two angels appeared at my front door. My grandmother and Aunt Bud walked in asking if I needed help.

"Help? Oh yes. Yes, yes, yes. I need help. Help would be wonderful."

At the time, my grandmother and Aunt Bud were 80 and 76 years old respectively. They wanted to take the girls to lunch at McDonald's, then to a nearby park to play.

"Oh that would be great!" I exclaimed. "Thank you, thank you, thank you. You are both lifesavers!" Off they went with Barney remaining on the back porch.

I tried cutting the carpet with my left hand, then back with my right hand—cutting, slicing and pushing—until both the living and dining room carpets finally lay flat.

Our heavy living room sleeper/sofa was carried in next and I plopped down on it, dripping wet and totally exhausted. Lamps, tables and more living and dining room furniture were then brought in.

Around noon, John walked in the front door. I was still on the couch.

Surveying the living and dining rooms, his face lit up. "Whoa, look at this! The movers are doing a terrific job, aren't they? Look what they've accomplished already!"

I didn't say a word. John looked over at me. "I'm impressed by how well you've managed everything and that you've even found time to relax on the couch. That's great."

I was numb and just stared at him.

He sat down next to me and started telling me about the temperomandibular joint lecture he had just heard.

I wasn't listening. I kept wondering if John was home for lunch. No, surely not. He couldn't be. **LUNCH????**

You know, you marry for Better or Worse. You marry in Sickness and in Health. You marry for the Good Times and the Bad Times. But the day you move into a house, you *never, ever,* ***EVER*** marry FOR LUNCH!!

෴

Mr. Allen

As I settled into the role as the wife of a student again—the third time in eight years—John and I together settled into something entirely new ... home ownership. And with that came something else ... the Art of Belt Tightening.

Our home cost $46,000. Although our VA loan did not require a down payment, we had to pay our mortgage lender one point—$4,600—which just about depleted our savings. Once that was done, we got a mortgage at 9½% interest. Remember those days? **OUCH!**

Because the Air Force was paying for John's dental school education, he had agreed to a reduction in rank and pay. John had been informed that under this Air Force sponsorship, he would automatically be promoted to 1st lieutenant at the start of his junior year and automatically promoted to captain upon graduation. This was all welcome news, but first, we had to get through these next two years under greatly reduced circumstances.

Going from captain back down to 2nd lieutenant again, his salary dropped from $16,128 a year to $11,976. **DOUBLE OUCH!**

John's monthly take-home pay was $890.25. Our monthly mortgage payment was $517.74. We were left with exactly $372.51 to live on per month and quickly learned that 'it don't go far'!

One of the first things we bought was an awl. We knew that we had to live more frugally in every way and that we would need to poke extra holes in our belts to cinch them tighter. "Skimp, Make Do or Do Without" became our motto.

When we eventually enrolled Jennifer and Betsy in school, we were told that because of John's salary, we qualified for welfare and were given lunch tokens. School lunches were 50¢ but they only cost 15¢ with a token. Except on very rare occasions, I always made the girls' lunches.

There were times when John told me that we were down to $13 in our checking account, which had to last until his next payday ... nine days away. With my cupboard almost bare, I still had to shop for groceries. Marked down "Day Old Bread" became a regular item on my list.

Winters are cold in New Jersey and fuel oil was at an all-time high. I set our thermostat to 62° during the day to conserve on heat and money. Even though I wore turtlenecks and sweaters in the house, when my fingertips started turning blue, I put on my old faux-fur black hat and my old quilted gold coat. If friends rang my front doorbell, they thought I was on my way out.

We survived of course, but we were sooooo poor!

How poor were we?????

Remember our motto 'Make do or do without'? In order to tell this story, I need to rewind.

I started high school in 1957 when I was 13. The high school had just hired a fellow by the name of Norman Allen, a brand-spankin'-new music teacher/choral director who had just graduated from college a few months before. He was probably 21, eight years older than I was. (In other words, ancient ☺).

When he learned that I played the piano, Mr. Allen asked me to be the accompanist for the high school Chorus and the Melodiers, a select group of really good singers, mostly upperclassmen. He was also my music theory teacher and it was because of him that key signatures, sharps and flats, whole and half steps, finally made sense.

I was his accompanist during my sophomore year as well and if truth be told, I developed a crush on Mr. Allen. He was cute ... a big teddy bear ... kind and thoughtful. He never ended a rehearsal without thanking me first. He was an excellent teacher, an all-around nice guy, and a real gentleman.

He got engaged to his college sweetheart during my sophomore year and toward the end of that school year, in early June 1959, he told us that he had an announcement to make.

Even though he had thoroughly enjoyed his two years at our high school, he explained that due to another opportunity, he was leaving to become the choral director at the new Paramus High School, about twelve miles away.

To say that I was heartbroken is an understatement. I cried the rest of that day and the next. I was too choked up to wish him good luck on the very last day of school, so I just waved goodbye.

About a week later, I got a letter from Mr. Allen, which I still have. Dated June 19, 1959, there is a 4¢ stamp on the envelope.

"Sherri –

"Even though I consider myself the world's worst letter writer, I thought that it would be better to say what I have to say in a letter instead of doing it in person.

As a teacher, it would be impossible for me to leave this job without trying, in some way, to thank you for everything you have done for me. Perhaps to some people playing a piano seems like a very small thing, but to someone who sings or conducts, it is a very vital part of his work and to have someone who you know you can always depend on is something that is treasured by anyone in this business. You are, without a doubt, the finest choral accompanist I have ever had the fortunate pleasure of working with. Now granted, I have not had a great many, but this makes little difference to me because besides being a pianist, you are a musician and too often these things do not go together.

It has been a great pleasure to work with you and I hope that sometime I will be able, in some small way, to repay you for the great amount of time you have spent during these two years helping to prepare the Chorus and Melodiers.

The very best of everything in the future.

Norman Allen

Well, after reading that I cried all over again. His letter became one of my high school treasures.

Fast-forward six years:

On Friday, April 23, 1965, I gave my college senior organ recital on the magnificent four-manual pipe organ in our beautiful Voorhees Chapel at Douglass College, the culmination of my four years as a music major.

Because my parents and grandmother all worked fulltime, I scheduled my recital for 8:30 p.m. that night, in order to give them enough time to drive the forty miles from Ridgefield Park to New Brunswick.

John and I, not yet engaged, had made hand-written invitations and sent them to family members, college friends and music professors. To let him know that I still thought about him, I sent one to Mr. Allen. He was still teaching at Paramus High School but I hadn't seen him since that last day of school in 1959.

My one-hour recital was followed by a reception with light refreshments in the Music Building auditorium, about a half-mile from the chapel. It was almost 10 p.m. by the time John and I, riding on his Honda motor scooter, got there.

When I walked into the auditorium, I got the surprise of my life. There stood Mr. Allen! He had driven all the way down from Paramus, at least an hour's drive, to come to my recital. His being there and making that effort is something I never forgot.

Now, where was I when I started this chapter? Oh yes, I remember.

Fast forward ten years later, to the spring of 1975. We were living in Teaneck and were as poor as church mice.

John was winding up his first year of dental school and had done very well considering that he had never majored in the biological sciences nor had he been a pre-dental undergrad.

I had been trying really hard to live within our means on a very limited income and was pleased that, so far, I had. Budgeting and being extra careful about spending money was on my mind constantly. I have never been much of a shopper but there were times when being resourceful came in handy.

Take, for example, the day that John, the girls and I went to church in Tenafly.

Sometime during that spring of 1975, my mother had called to tell me that she had just learned that Mr. Allen was the choir director at the First Presbyterian Church in Tenafly, a town about ten miles from our house.

I immediately decided that I wanted John, the girls and me to attend their 11 o'clock service that coming Sunday. It was going to be *my* turn to surprise Mr. Allen.

Wanting to impress Mr. Allen with our family, I got the girls all dressed up in their Sunday best. I decided to wear an Easter suit that I'd had for years.

I got out a pair of taupe seamed stockings (remember those days, trying to keep the seams straight?), then started rummaging through my underwear drawer looking for my girdle. At the time, I didn't own pantyhose and couldn't have afforded them anyway. They were expensive ... $9.99!

Hunting for my girdle, I pushed my pajamas and undies from one side of my dresser drawer to the other but could I find it? No! Where was it? I checked other dresser drawers but nope, I didn't see it anywhere. My girdle was gone.

Then it dawned on me. I had thrown it away the year before when we lived in Wisconsin. Darn it all. I had had it since high school. It was old, torn and two of its garters had pulled off. Good grief, now what was I going to do? How the heck was I going to hold my stockings up?

Even though stockings and a girdle were the proper attire to wear when dressing up, I hated wearing them, *hated it!* I don't like wearing anything tight. For me, squeezing into a girdle was like trying to yank a rubber band up the trunk of an oak tree ... impossible!

I have never been too thin and have always had solid legs too. I hate jamming my legs into tight stockings that then resemble the casing on sausages.

But back to my girdle dilemma.

I thought about my situation for a moment, wondering what I could do, when a light bulb popped on over my head.

I ran into Betsy's room and grabbed six diaper pins.

Even though both girls were out of diapers, I had kept their diaper pins for quick fixes—hemming jeans, shortening curtains, reattaching coat buttons—whatever. Betsy Ross I ain't.

Coming up with what I thought was a creative solution, I pinned the diaper pins, three to a side, around each of my legs at the bottom of my nylon undies. They would act as garters.

Then pulling up my stockings, I pinned the top of each to my undies via the diaper pins.

Voilá! Problem solved. Who needed a girdle anyway?

I recreated my "invention" for this chapter and had John take this picture, a poor woman's answer to a girdle:

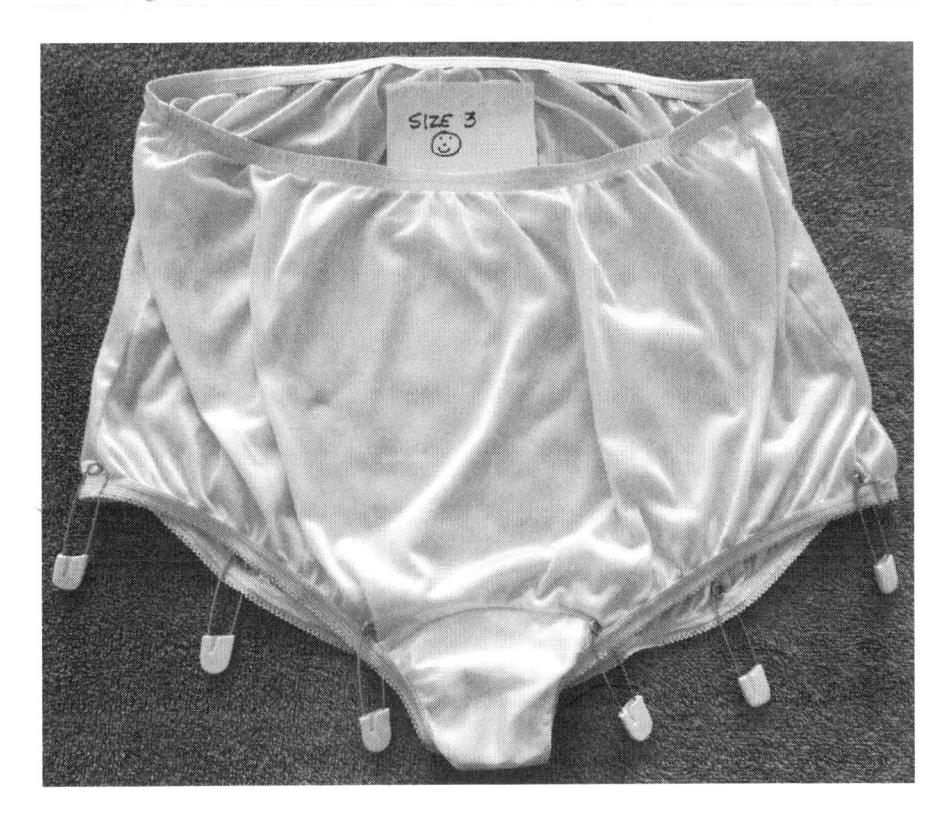

Quite proud of my solution, we got to the Presbyterian Church in Tenafly before 11 o'clock, found an empty pew in the middle of the sanctuary and a few minutes later, the service began.

Looking stylish and feeling almost like a schoolgirl again, I could hardly wait to see Mr. Allen and the surprise that awaited him ... Me!

The choir sang an Introit from the narthex, then started their two-by-two processional down the center aisle, women first.

Sure enough, following the basses, Mr. Allen brought up the rear in his choir director's robe. He was as cute as ever but he was looking straight ahead towards the altar. He didn't see me but watching him made me smile and tear up.

We sang the first hymn, read the Responsive Readings, sang the "Gloria Patri" and listened to scripture from the Old Testament.

In standing to sing the next hymn, "The Church's One Foundation", I suddenly became aware that ... Oh my GOSH, NOOOOOOOOO!!! ... something had moved.

My undies started falling down!!!

Trying not to panic with *my* foundation crumbling, I slowly put my hymnal in one hand and with the other, hooked my thumb into the waistband of my skirt. I was able to grab the top of my undies and carefully pull them back up to my waist. Whew, I was never so glad to finally sing "Aah-men".

Ten minutes later, when I stood for the "Doxology", my undies dropped again, this time to my belly button.

Good GRIEF, this was terrible! My undies were too thin and the material was too flimsy. They didn't constrict me the way a girdle would have. They could not hold my diaper-pinned stockings up tightly enough and the diaper pins did not secure my stockings firmly enough. I was wearing Rube Goldberg underpants and everything pulled down each time I stood up.

What was I going to do? What *could* I do?

This time I couldn't reach my undies with my thumb so I tried hiking them up through my clothes with my elbows, a la James Cagney in a gangster movie.

I broke out in a cold sweat. John looked over at me and arched an eyebrow, as if asking, "What the heck is going on?" I shook my head back and forth and thought ... nothing is going *ON*, something is coming *OFF!!*

With the organ introduction to the final hymn in the service, "Stand up, stand up for Jesus", I took a deep breath, said a little prayer, stood up and my undies dropped to the middle of my thighs.

I didn't move.

I didn't sing.

I froze in place and stood there like a statue.

Barely breathing, I clamped my legs together as tightly as I could. I looked down at my sagging, bunched-up stockings below my skirt and saw that they looked like a Chinese Shar-Pei dog:

The service ended and the choir filed out through a side door.

Knock-kneed and bent over, I waddled out of the pew and inched my way toward the back of the church. Seeing a sign to a Ladies Room, I whispered to John that I had a problem and that I would be out as soon as possible.

My palms were sweaty and my hands shook as I unfastened the diaper pins. I took my stockings off and stuffed everything into my purse. Then I pulled my undies back up to my waist, where they were supposed to be. Waves of relief washed over me.

We found the choir room. As I walked towards Mr. Allen, his eyebrows shot up and his face lit up. "SHERRI!" he cried out as he scooped me up in a great big bear hug.

It was a wonderful way to end that morning but if the last hymn had been "Just as I Am", I had another verse:

♪ Just as I am, ♪
Oh Lord, one plea -
Please keep my undies
UP for me!

♋♋

Artichoke Spinach Casserole - 1975

Artichoke Spinach Casserole
Ingredients • Three or four 10-ounce boxes of chopped spinach • Two 14-ounce cans artichoke hearts, drained and split in half • One stick margarine, melted • One 8-ounce package of cream cheese, softened • Seasonings – Add garlic salt, pepper and oregano, to taste • One cup bread crumbs, or enough to make a one-quarter inch layer on top of casserole.
Instructions: • Preheat Oven to 350° • Cook spinach, drain. Mix spinach, margarine, cream cheese and seasonings. • Line a glass 8"x8" baking dish with artichoke halves. • Pour a layer of spinach on top and repeat, placing another layer of artichokes and then top with spinach. • Sprinkle bread crumbs over the top. Cover. • Place in 350° oven for 30 minutes. For crispy bread crumbs, remove cover for the last 5-10 minutes. • YIELD: 8 servings.

In November of 1975, John's parents offered to host a family Thanksgiving dinner in their home in Princeton. There would be fourteen of us in all.

I offered to make four dozen pumpkin muffins that our family loved. I also said that I would make a delicious vegetable dish that I had made in the past, an artichoke-spinach casserole.

I bought all the necessary ingredients weeks ahead of time and the Saturday before Thanksgiving, I made, baked and froze 48 pumpkin muffins.

I had decided to double the artichoke-spinach recipe, so I bought EIGHT 10-ounce boxes of frozen chopped spinach, FOUR 14-ounce cans of artichoke hearts, TWO 8-ounce packages of cream cheese, I would use TWO sticks of margarine, TWO cups of bread crumbs and double my seasonings. A low-cal dish it ain't but um, umm, yummm ... it is good!

The Tuesday before Thanksgiving was the perfect day to make the casserole since the girls and John were still in school and I had the afternoon to myself. And because I had room in my refrigerator, I could keep the casserole there until we drove the 60 miles to Princeton on Thanksgiving morning.

As I worked in the kitchen getting out all the necessary ingredients, I noticed that the floor was dirty and needed a thorough mopping—a good project to do while foot traffic was at a minimum.

I put some water in my Dutch oven, then ripped open and put in the eight boxes of frozen chopped spinach—eight solid green bricks. (I need to mention that this was before the days of microwave ovens and before I learned I could have thawed the spinach ahead of time.)

In any case, I set my Dutch oven on my stove over a low flame and adjusted the lid a little to let steam escape while it cooked. I figured that would take about half an hour.

Next order of business: Tackle the floor.

Carrying kitchen chairs into the dining room and throwing kitchen mats on our back porch, I filled the kitchen sink with hot water and liquid floor detergent. I then grabbed my sponge mop. Mopping one section of the floor at a time, the water in the sink was soon filthy with grit, grime, pieces of dead brown leaves and Barney's hair.

Our kitchen was small and it didn't take long to clean, so I sat down in our living room to read as I waited for the floor to dry. That only took 15 minutes and the spinach was cooked as well.

I grabbed two potholders and carrying the very heavy Dutch oven over to the sink, I saw that I hadn't emptied the sink of the filthy brown mop water. Oh well, no problem. I just needed to drain the cooked spinach.

I slid the lid of the pot back a little to pour off the water. Holding the lid in position with my thumbs and the potholders, I tilted the Dutch oven over the dirty water. Boiling water came pouring out which made the pot extremely hot to hold even with potholders.

YEEEEEEEOW!

Standing at an awkward angle, I kept tilting the Dutch oven over further and further to drain it completely.

Have you ever tried draining cooked spinach? You can't. It is impossible. It never drains completely, much like a woman who's had too many cups of coffee and needs to frequent a bathroom.

I was pressing the pot lid so tightly to keep it in place that my thumbs started to ache and my arms started to shake. Grimacing, I kept holding the tilted pot and the water kept coming, coming, coming when suddenly, the lid slipped and fell off into the filthy mop water followed by the entire pot of spinach ... **KerPLOP!!!**

For a moment, I just stood there in shock. Then I started jumping up and down, like I was on a pogo stick!

"NO!NO!NO!NO!NO!NO!NO!NO!NO!NO!NO!NO!NO!"

I couldn't believe it. All eight boxes of cooked spinach were now *GARBAGE*. I felt sick ... I *was* sick!

Good GRIEF! Now what? I needed to buy eight more boxes of frozen chopped spinach right away.

Grabbing my coat and purse, I drove to Pathmark, our nearest grocery store. With my mind reeling, I never noticed the school zone speed limit sign:

SCHOOL ZONE
15mph
8am-9am and 3pm-4pm

The next thing I knew, I saw a red light flashing in my rearview mirror. I looked at the clock on my dashboard ... 3:02 p.m.

I pulled over as did the police car. The police officer had clocked me doing 25mph in the 15mph school zone. I was two minutes too late.

Chopped spinach cost 39¢ a box in 1975 so I paid $3.12 for another eight boxes. Adding in the price of the cans of artichoke hearts, the packages of cream cheese, the sticks of margarine and the bread crumbs PLUS my speeding ticket, the cost of my delicious artichoke spinach casserole came to $66.58.

Does anyone have a good recipe for spinach and mop water?

CR☙

Barney Cards

John completed his second year of dental school successfully and as promised, at the start of his junior year, he was promoted to 1st lieutenant.

While that little bit of extra money in his paycheck helped, we were barely getting by. Our Art of Belt Tightening wasn't tight enough and we needed to dip into our meager savings too often just to meet expenses. I decided that I needed to find a part time job.

Contacting the American Guild of Organists, I discovered that the Neighborhood Reformed Church in Ridgefield Park, my hometown, was looking for an organist/choir director. I applied for the job and was hired.

The job only paid $45 a week but it was just what I needed. The church was only a ten-minute drive from our house so I could practice during the week when the girls were in school. John could sing in the choir, too, provided he passed the audition, that is. ☺

A few months later with a little more money coming in, we started tackling other house projects. John, ever the handyman, wanted a den—a place where he could get away to study. The only room in our house big enough to create a den was our bedroom. It was as wide as our house and the room was bigger than we needed.

John partitioned our bedroom into two rooms, two-thirds of the space for our bedroom, the other third for his den. He placed studs every sixteen inches on center from floor to ceiling and framed a doorway. Placing 4x8-foot sections of sheetrock, he taped and floated the drywall, hung a door and matched the existing room's baseboard on both sides of the wall. We then painted our bedroom and the new den a pretty blue and painted the door, trim and baseboards white.

I hope you are impressed with my construction lingo! Actually, I asked John to describe what he did and this is what he said. Whoever heard of floating a drywall for heaven's sakes??

Our next project was to paint and wallpaper the kitchen, giving it a fresh look, before tackling our basement. Half of our basement was taken up by the monstrous fuel oil tank, our washer and dryer and John's workbench.

With our girls needing more room to play, John decided to "finish" the other half. He walled off that half of the basement, wired in overhead fluorescent lighting, installed a drop-in acoustical tile ceiling and paneled the room in faux knotty pine. Indoor-outdoor carpeting completed the room.

While John does a great job as our barbeque Grillmeister, he can't cook worth a darn in my kitchen and makes an incredible mess if he tries. He's also a Clutter Bug of the First Order, but he sure is handy ... and dandy!

In 1976, while thinking of other ways to earn money, it occurred to me that perhaps Barney could play a role.

Barney was just the best when it came to playing "statue", staying put when we told him to "Stay". Whatever I told him to do ... to lie down and put his head down or to sit and put a paw up on a chair or whatever I had him wear ... when I said 'Stay' he did just that, remaining stock-still until I said "Okay."

I came up with an idea that ... if I do say so myself ... was really ahead of its time. I wanted to create Barney Cards, greeting cards with our Barney decked out in crazy outfits with funny captions. As far as I knew, there was nothing like it on the market and I thought the cards could possibly be a big hit.

Jotting down various ideas, I rummaged through our props suitcase and assembled an assortment of items to put on "Mr. B" (one of our many 'terms of endearment' for him). I knew that as soon as my "Barney Cards" hit the market that Hallmark would beat a path to my door and make me an offer I couldn't refuse!

I decided that the first couple of pictures would use no props at all. I would just have funny captions written underneath Barney's picture. Here he is:

Long time
no see!

Just because we
don't see eye-to-eye
can't we still be
friends?

Gradually I added a prop or two while John clicked picture after picture. Barney was most cooperative.

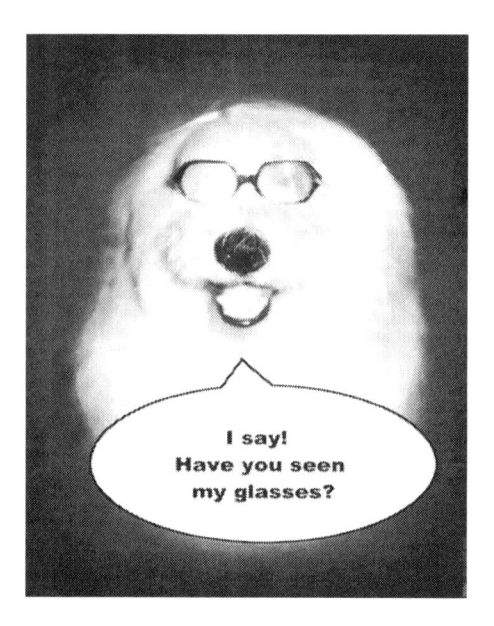

I say! Have you seen my glasses?

Life is cold and empty without you

Oooh ... doesn't he look sad?

Please keep in mind that we had no professional equipment. We didn't have the proper lighting or a wardrobe department. This was just our "Mom and Pop" effort, working on a shoestring budget.

I had bought myself a brown wig back in 1971 and had only worn it once. I got it out and 'styled' it on Barney's head.

Then I found a beret in the props suitcase. Barney thought he was a French poodle:

Now I need to fast-forward to the year 2006—twenty years later.

We were living in Lake Oswego, Oregon, a suburb of Portland. One morning I got a real shocker while reading the *Oregonian,* our Portland daily newspaper. The paper featured a story that day about a bulldog named Zelda and I could not believe what I was reading.

Zelda in the news...

EXTRA! EXTRA!

The Oregonian

Portland's role-playing bulldog is a natural card. Tuesday, December 26, 2006. Zelda is a 10-year-old Portland bulldog of, uh, unconventional beauty who graces a line of greeting cards, gift books and calendars. She dispenses pithy gems of wisdom with the help of her human soul mate and interpreter, Carol Gardner.

This dog may be one of the most popular pooches on the planet right now. There is a line of 82 greeting cards sold at Hallmark stores. There is a series of "Zelda Wisdom" books. Her image has even been licensed internationally.

It all started out when this pooch and her owner were underdogs. It was 1997, and the darkest time of Gardner's life. She was 52, going through a "nasty divorce," jobless and in debt.

Gardner's divorce attorney joked to her client that she should get therapy … or a dog. She opted for a puppy. "I always wanted a bulldog, because they made me laugh. I named her Zelda because of the

'Z'," says Gardner. "I felt that what looked like the end might be the beginning." And it was.

When a friend told Gardner that Purina had a contest that gave the winner free dog food for a year, the cash-strapped former advertising creative director entered her dog. She put a Santa cap on Zelda and placed her in a bathtub filled with bubble bath. The caption: "For Christmas I got a dog for my husband ... good trade, huh?" Zelda's pithy view of divorce won the contest. Gardner got an idea. Why not develop a line of cards with Zelda as the star?

"No one had ever taken a live dog, given it a name and designed cards around it," says Gardner.

Zelda Wisdom cards went on sale in a few Portland stores and were an instant hit. Gardner is a savvy entrepreneur who used her advertising background and knack for publicity to create a hugely successful business from one puppy's appealing face.

******

Well, I have news for you, Ms. Gardner. I had taken my dog and designed cards around him. His name was Barney and he was FIRST, so there!

I was stunned. I could not believe what I had just read and wanted to scream. But, getting back to 1976, and as you see, Barney enjoyed being a model. No, make that a 'supermodel'.

This was his chance to show off his modeling 'chops' and he relished every minute, smiling in every picture.

There is no doubt in my mind that he and I were ahead of our time and we had great fun doing these fashion 'shoots'.

Lastly, here is one my favorite poses, taken when we lived at Loring Air Force Base in Maine in 1970, before I ever thought of Barney Cards. Say hello to "Groucho Barney"!

After developing these photos and seeing how amateurish they were, I came to a sad realization. My being able to make and market Barney Cards was a pipe dream.

We did not have the proper equipment, the right lighting, the best setting, the money required nor did John have the time to invest in the gamble that mass-producing these cards would have entailed. What was I thinking?

There was no way this was ever going to be a moneymaking venture. These photographs ended up in a shoebox and that was the end of it. I had a great idea at the wrong time in our lives. I surely missed a Golden Opportunity.

Here's a photo of our handsome boy, Mr. B.

Barney was such a terrific dog ... a dear, sweet, loving companion. We enjoyed his wonderful company for another five years, until his health began to fail. Barney died of age-related infirmities on October 28, 1981. He was twelve years old and the day he died remains one of the saddest days in our lives. John and I will always miss him.

Gettysburg

My daughters say it is all *my* fault. I'm the one to blame for John's being a photoholic! If I hadn't given him that Kodak Instamatic camera for a wedding present back in 1966, we would have had more closet space and been younger.

Younger? Yes, younger!

Jennifer, Betsy and I have waited hundreds of hours, *countless* hours, for John to take a picture.

It wasn't so bad when John used the Kodak Instamatic camera. He would take a picture quickly, efficiently, *instantly*.

But over time he bought better, more sophisticated cameras. With each new camera, each with more dials than the previous one, more time was spent waiting. We girls would wait and wait and wait because John wanted to take *just* the right shot at *just* the right angle in *just* the right light. Yes, years spent waiting, waiting, waiting—while I got older, older, older … my brown hair turning whiter, whiter, whiter.

We would have had more closet space, too, because John took thousands upon thousands of slides, stored them in cartons and stashed them in our closets—cartons on shelves in our closets, cartons on the floor of our closets, cartons containing three-ring binders filled with plastic sheets holding slides, slides still in the little boxes they were developed in, all tossed into cartons and put in our closets.

I have been tempted to put a large yellow highway sign up on our front door:

WARNING … SLIDE AREA!!!

We have more prints than the FBI.

The truly amazing thing is that even if John were to take the time to look at *any* of these prints and slides years later, he doesn't remember where they were taken and who is in them.

"When and where did I take this?" he asks, handing me a print.

"Hmmm, let's see," I say, studying the photograph. "Well," I drawl, "that's our base townhouse in the background when we were stationed at Stewart Air Force Base. The trees are green. I am *not* pregnant, so, umm, that would be the summer of 1968."

"Oh, good," he replies. "And who is that couple standing next to you?"

"Your parents."

And lenses? We've got short ones, long ones, skinny ones, fat ones. Each comes in its own separate lens case. Cameras, camera cases, lenses, lens cases, camera bags, tripods, both slide and print film and video cassettes. It is mind-boggling.

John bought our first video camera back in the early 1980s when they were just becoming popular. The accompanying battery pack was the size of a suitcase and weighed a ton. When John slung that battery pack over his left shoulder, he listed to port. It was so large and cumbersome that it looked like he was carrying around his own heart-lung machine.

I didn't mind a few photos at first but this little hobby had gotten way out of hand.

And John never takes just one shot. Oh no. What if it doesn't come out? Heaven forbid! No, John has to take multiple shots of the same thing from different vantage points, using different focal-stops or shutter speeds and under the constantly changing conditions of available light. You get the picture. We stand and wait, we sit and wait, we wait and wait.

Whenever I started looking forward to a vacation, I would remember. "Oh that's right, here we go again. Another opportunity to take more pictures." *Any* vacation for me was like buying a gun ... a seven-day vacation included a three-day waiting period.

John will take a picture of anything that strikes his fancy. Family and friends? Sure, great! Pretty scenery? Hmmm, okay but just take one picture, thank you. Handsome statues? Well, if you must. But squirrels, ducks, or seagulls? Pah-LEEZE!

Oooooh, I got so mad that sometimes I would ... I would ... well, let me tell you what I did.

There was no dental school during the summer months so when we had a little extra money and time allowed, we took short, family vacations when we weren't working on house projects.

Because money was tight and staying in a motel was out of the question, we were able to borrow a camper from John's parents, the kind where the camper sits in the bed of a pickup truck. It was small and efficient and it was the only way we could afford to get away.

On these vacations, the girls would ride in the camper lying on the big bed above the truck's roof, over the cab, looking out at the road ahead through its front window.

Barney always went with us on our vacations but he preferred to ride up front with us. He liked to sit in the middle of the bench seat between John and me and share his head in each of our laps.

On this particular get-away, we headed south to Virginia and the Skyline Drive. I had read what a beautiful drive it was and we wanted to see some of the area. We camped in Front Royal, Virginia, at the northern end of the Skyline Drive, our first night out. Thumbing through a free brochure from the campground office, I read: "The Skyline Drive is one of the most spectacular scenic highways in the East. The awesomely beautiful drive runs north to south, where frequent overlooks afford spectacular views of the area's mountains, valleys, streams and distant vistas."

It sounded nice but *frequent* overlooks? *How* frequent?

The Skyline Drive is 105 miles long and has 75 overlooks. SEVENTY FIVE??? Since the drive runs north and south, the overlooks face east and west. We set out early the next morning. The summer sun was shining brightly as we drove up and onto the Skyline Drive and headed south. We were immediately enclosed in a tunnel of trees—a wall of trees to our left and right, their branches intertwining above us, over the road.

With trees bordering the road, the only thing we could see was … trees. The road, with one lane of traffic in each direction, meandered and we crawled along at the posted 35mph. We did not see one other car.

We got to the first overlook, a left turn down a little slope into the parking area behind the tree line. No one else was around. John grabbed his camera, I put Barney on his leash and the girls got out of the camper.

We walked over to a low stone wall and could just make out hazy mounds of mountains in the distance. We were facing east and the sun was shining in our eyes, blinding us.

While John climbed over the stone wall to take a picture, the girls and I stood there looking at a view that was completely washed out by the sun. We squinted at mountain forms in the distance while John took two pictures. CLICK. CLICK.

Jennifer and Betsy got bored and started doing cartwheels and backbends in the parking lot. Barney lay down on the macadam.

"Okay girls, back in the camper." I ordered. "Where's your father?"

They pointed. "Oh," I said, looking to my left. "JOHN!" I yelped.

He was standing on the stone wall at the far end of the parking lot in front of a plunging drop-off. He was balanced on one leg because he had his camera bag tucked between his knees. He had one hand shielding the camera lens from the sun and with the other, was taking pictures of the haze. CLICK. CLICK.

"Good GRIEF," I shouted. "Are you nuts? That's dangerous!" He was scaring the heck out of me. "It's all hazy and washed out!" I shouted. "Wait'll we get to the next overlook."

We all piled back into the camper, pulled out of the parking area and continued south for a quarter of a mile when we came upon another overlook, this time to the right.

We pulled down into the parking area and got out. John grabbed his camera, I put Barney on his leash and the girls got out of the camper. We walked down to another low stone wall but this time, facing west and with the sun now behind us, the view was crystal clear with tree-covered mountains in front of us and leafy green valleys below with gurgling streams. This was much better. CLICK. CLICK.

We got back in the camper and craaaawled 35mph to the next lookout, only a half a mile farther down the road. It was also to the right, again facing west. We parked the camper, got out and looked. It was the identical view that we had just seen a half-mile back. CLICK. CLICK.

"JOHN! What are you doing?" I asked incredulously. "Why are you taking more shots of the *same* view?"

"Because the sun is not hiding behind the clouds this time."

At the 11th overlook, the girls did not want to get out of the camper anymore. "C'mon girls. You need to get out and stretch your legs." I said brightly. "C'mon. Maybe you'll see a chipmunk!"

"We don't care," they chimed in unison. "We don't *waaant* to see chipmunks."

"Well, I care. C'mon. Out." CLICK. CLICK.

We drove another mile to another overlook. CLICK. CLICK.

We drove south, turned right and faced west. CLICK. CLICK. We drove south, turned left and faced east. CLICK. CLICK. It *all* looked the same.

There was very little traffic, yet we drove at a snail's pace, hemmed in along a tree-lined road that offered no views whatsoever.

By the 17th overlook, the girls *refused* to get out of the camper. When I went to put on his leash, even Barney wouldn't budge! "Grrrrrrr." (That's Barney, not me!).

By then, I had had it, too, and to heck with the view. We had seen what there was to see. I didn't want to look at any more mountains. I didn't care about another vista, valley or stream. I got back in the camper and Barney fell asleep on my lap.

We went to almost all 75 overlooks. We drove. We parked. We waited and waited and waited and waited while John shot picture after picture. We waited so long that I swear, some of the trees were starting to turn their autumn colors, red and yellow! It drove me nuts. The only thing I wanted to shoot was ... well, never mind.

Needless to say, by the time we exited the Skyline Drive, things had gotten very quiet in our cab. We then turned north to drive to Gettysburg in Pennsylvania where we camped just outside of town. We rolled into Gettysburg the next morning.

Stopping first at the Visitors Center, our eyes panned across the Cyclorama Painting, a huge forty-two-foot high panorama depicting the Battle of Gettysburg.

Next, it was on to a large display called the 'electric map'. Looking down at this topographical map from bleacher seats and listening to a recording, the narrator told us what had taken place during the Battle of Gettysburg, July 1st-3rd, 1863.

As each battle and skirmish was described, that area on the electric map lit up with little white lights: Cemetery Ridge, Little Round Top, Pickett's Charge.

It was absolute carnage. 75,000 Confederate troops and 88,000 Union troops met and fought. In three days of fighting, 51,000 men and boys were either killed, wounded or were missing.

The recording droned on and on, giving endless statistics and battle sequences. When John started clipping his fingernails, I knew it was time to move on.

We set off to drive through the park and around the battlefields. The weather was picture perfect and at first we stopped at every cannon, every statue and every monument. CLICK. CLICK.

As we drove along, I began reading one of the brochures that we had picked up at the Visitors Center and almost went into cardiac arrest. There were over 1,400 monuments, canon and memorials in the park. 1,400??? Oh, Lawdy!

After a few more cannon and monument shots, John decided that he wanted to take some artsy shots. Seeing rows of canons lined up like soldiers at attention, his camera went CLICK. CLICK.

Then John noticed a statue of a Union soldier holding a rifle up over his head. John wanted to take a picture of him silhouetted against the American flag hanging limply on the other side of the road. John wanted the flag to unfurl for this artsy shot so while he adjusted his lens, we waited. There was no breeze. We waited some more. He crouched down to take the picture looking up at the soldier, the flag in the background. His nose was pressed against the camera ... wait, wait, wait ... finally, there was a slight breeze; the flag started unfurling ... wait ... wait ... "John? JOHN? **JOHN!!! TAKE THE—**" CLICK. CLICK. CLICK.

A Regimental monument. CLICK. CLICK. A statue of a Confederate soldier on horseback, CLICK, another statue, CLICK, endless clicks.

Finally, I couldn't take it *any* longer. I decided that I had to "Fight fire with fire". I came up with a plan. Of *course!* Why hadn't I thought of this before ... like 759 rolls of film ago? I would give John a taste of his own medicine. See how *he* liked waiting. Oh yes, this was going to be sweet. Suh-WEEET!

It was approaching lunchtime so we pulled into a playground/picnic area. The girls jumped out of the camper and made a beeline for the swings and seesaw.

Dogs were not allowed in the picnic area so Barney stayed in the cab. We rolled down both the driver- and passenger-windows all the way so Barney would have plenty of fresh air.

"John, would you give me the camera, please."

"Huh? What about lunch?"

"Yeah, I'll get lunch in a little while," I said. "Right now I need the camera."

"What for?"

I pointed. "I saw something, back behind that monument over there, just as we pulled in. I want to get some pictures of it."

"What? What is it? I'll take the pictures for you."

"No, no. This is my idea, my pictures. You wait here and look after the girls and Barney. I don't want him jumping out of the cab. Just wait here and I'll be back as soon as I take the pictures.

I had John show me how to use the camera again, which dials to adjust and how to focus properly. I then walked back down the road to the monument and got behind it. I found a spot where I could still see the camper but John could not see me. I sat down on the grass and looked at my watch. It was 11:30 a.m.

I listened to the birds chirp away. I stared up at the sky. I peeked around the monument and saw John sitting on the running board. Barney had moved over to the open window on the driver's side. He was sitting behind the steering wheel, looking out the window. 11:40 a.m. Oh yes, this was perfect. Make *John* wait. See how *he* likes it!

I watched cars and other campers drive into the picnic area. I uncrossed my legs because they were starting to fall asleep.

11:55 a.m. I saw John starting to pace. He kept looking in the direction of the monument but he couldn't see me. Yes John, now it's *your* turn to wonder what the *HECK* is taking soooo long.

I looked more carefully at the monument in front of me and read some of the names of the soldiers and the states they were from. It was noon. I had been gone for half an hour.

I got up, backed away from the monument and disappeared into a grove of trees behind the monument. I could no longer see John but now I had to find something to photograph. Hmmm, what? what?? As I worked my way through the trees, I came out to a small rose garden. Perfect! I'll take some photos of a rose ... a picture-perfect Pennsylvania posy.

I circled around looking for a rosebud and found a red beauty. Ah, *my* artsy shots. Kneeling down, I checked my dials, my focus and had the sun coming over my shoulder. I zoomed in. CLICK. CLICK. I circled around the rose bush and took a few more shots of the bud from the other side. CLICK. CLICK.

I looked at my watch. It was 12:15 p.m. I had been gone for *forty-five minutes.* Yessiree, fight fire with fire.

I turned around and headed back towards the picnic area. I was giddy with anticipation. I could hardly *wait* to see John's face and *his* reaction when I finally strolled back to the camper. Let him cool his heels and wait for me ... HA! *Revenge* at last!

When the picnic area came into view, I circled around to come in behind the camper so that John would not see me approaching.

Yes, there was John standing by the driver's side but ... WAIT A MINUTE!! What was **THIS?**

Barney was standing on the cab seat, his head hanging out of the driver's side window. His bobtail was wagging back and forth excitedly, a mile-a-minute. John was standing next to him, patting his head and chatting away.

Two young gals in madras shorts, Lacoste tennis shirts and sockless Bass Weejuns were standing next to Barney, laughing and talking to both John and Barney. John later confirmed my suspicion. They were co-eds from nearby Gettysburg College. I could just make out what they were saying:

"… n't he just the *cutest*, Mary! How long have you had him?"

"What soft ears he has! Oh my gosh, he is *so* handsome!"

"What a cute name … Barney!"

When I finally appeared and John saw me, he jumped back about a foot, glanced at his watch and said, "Oh *Hi*, hon! Back so *soon?*"

Would you know … do straitjackets come in periwinkle?

ଔଓ

What Space Between My Front Teeth?

The first time I ever saw John was the evening of my third day at college in 1961.[1] Dr. Mason Gross, the president of Rutgers University, was hosting a reception for all incoming Rutgers University and Douglass College freshmen at his university home in New Brunswick, New Jersey.

I had no idea who John was that evening but I noticed him talking to another Douglass freshman gal I had just met the day before.

Looking at him from a distance and in profile, John looked kind of cute so I circled around other groups of freshmen to get a closer look. And when I did, I came to a complete standstill. What a shock! John had a huge space between his two front teeth! I mean, look at his Alfred E. Neuman smile. It's really something, isn't it? All he needed were "jug" ears and freckles on his nose!

"Thay! Have you 'theen' my diastema?"

Yes, John, we do.

I learned later that a natural space between any two adjacent teeth is called a diastema (pronounced "die-AS-tuh-ma"). John had a prize-winning beauty, don't you think? This photo was taken in 1974 when John was thirty-one, but he looked just like this in college.

The thing is, John never saw his diastema as a detriment to his appearance. In fact, he never even thought about it until I came along!

---

[1] *Don't Set the Alarm!*

When bringing up the topic, John just referred to the "gap-toothed" English actor, Terry Thomas, who claimed that his diastema meant that he was very "passionate"!

We know today that John was in good company with many others including ... David Letterman, Madonna, Elton John and model Lauren Hutton, all sharing in this "passionate" quality!

As John liked to boast, it wasn't just anyone who could take in a mouthful of water while swimming on his back and squirt water ten-feet up in the air through that gap like a veritable Old Faithful! That took talent!

Speaking of which, Fairleigh Dickinson's Dental School had a Talent Show every year in the spring. Anyone who had a "talent" could be in the show. In other words, anyone who could sing, dance, juggle, do magic, wiggle their ears or swallow a goldfish was welcome! One fellow actually did swallow a goldfish as his "talent" one year!

John signed up to be in the show his freshman year. While I accompanied him on the piano, John sang "Misty" in the Johnny Mathis voice and style, even going up to that high note entrance on the reprise ... "Ooooooooon my own...".

Well, let me tell you, John brought down the house. What an ovation! It was thrilling. John decided then and there that he wanted to be in the Dental School Talent Show *every* year.

The next year, in looking through our record albums, we found John Denver's "Greatest Hits" with John Denver's picture on the album cover.

John liked many of John Denver's music and decided to sing his popular song "Sunshine on My Shoulders".

So going through his closet and our props suitcase again, we pulled out this and that, and were able to put together an outfit for John to wear during his sophomore performance.

What was pretty amazing was that when John Rogerson put his props on, John Denver looked like he had a twin brother. The resemblance was quite remarkable, really uncanny!

Don't you agree?

The only way you can tell the two apart is John Rogerson's diastema!

Will the *Real* John Denver please stand up?

In 1977, during John's third year of dental school and at my urging, John thought that he might be able to improve his appearance by bringing his two front teeth closer together and at least reduce the size of his diastema.

Using orthodontic rubber bands, he wrapped them around his two front teeth to squeeze them closer together.

The plan worked except that only the crowns of his teeth were being brought together, not the roots.

As soon as the rubber bands were removed, the gap began to open up as his teeth tried to "right" themselves over their roots.

When you wear orthodontic braces, rubber bands move the entire tooth (crown and root) along the orthodontic wire rather than just tipping the teeth toward the empty space of a diastema.

After he graduated and we moved to Keesler AFB in Biloxi, Mississippi, John had orthodontic brackets and wires attached to his six front teeth. With this treatment, his two front teeth did come together in perfect alignment.

After the braces were removed, John wore a retainer for years to keep his front teeth from separating again.

Much later, when we were stationed at Sheppard AFB in Wichita Falls, Texas in the 1990s, another dentist allowed John's front teeth to open slightly. That dentist then closed the gap permanently by bonding a tooth-colored "porcelain" to each tooth, widening each incisor until the space was closed.

As John explained to me, he had resin placed on the *mesial* surfaces of central incisors #s 8 and 9.

And this, Ladies and Gentlemen, is the result:

"Thay! Did you know I 'youthed' to have a diastema?"

Yes John, we do, and you look mighty handsome in your official Air Force picture, taken in 1994.

John's diastema was gone at last and it has 'stayed gone' all these years. And all because he was accepted to dental school.

Dentoscope *1978*

Fairleigh Dickinson University's School of Dentistry yearbook was called the *Dentoscope*.

At a retirement party in 1977, John presented a retiring dental professor with a pen-and-ink portrait that John had drawn of him. Classmates of John's on the yearbook committee immediately took note. "Hey! This guy can draw!"

They asked John to join the *Dentoscope* staff for his Class of 1978. They wanted him to draw a portrait of every student in his class.

Oh really? And just how many would that be? How about 79!!

So, at the beginning of John's fourth and final year of dental school and despite the enormous demands on his time both academically and clinically, John accepted the challenge.

He decided to draw the faces of each of his classmates first and then add body caricatures.

After every classmate had had an official yearbook picture taken, John received a contact sheet of these graduation photos. Each picture was a greatly reduced, "thumbnail" size image–79 of them all on one sheet!

Unable to have each classmate pose for their portrait, John used the thumbnail photo instead. Needing to see each photo 'up close and personal', *very* up close, John had to wear his dental magnifying loops.

Dental magnifying loops, also worn by jewelers, are mounted on an adjustable headband and look like a pair of goggles where the lenses are magnifying glasses. The loops magnified his classmates' photos enough for John to see their faces in detail. He also had to have excellent lighting and a comfortable place in which to work. The den that John had built in our bedroom was the perfect place to do this project.

Wearing the loops and using a pencil, John began sketching each classmate's portrait. He drew and erased, drew and erased, until he felt he had captured the look of that person.

After he had sketched about a dozen faces, John noticed that each succeeding portrait was better than the previous one. The more he sketched, the more accurately he was able to capture his subject. So, dissatisfied with his initial drawings, he went back and drew the first twelve all over again. That only left 67 more to do!

It took months of drawing, hundreds of hours wearing those magnifying loops, but once he had drawn each classmate's face, John went back and drew their bodies, emphasizing a particular characteristic, interest or trait of that individual.

Being the class vice president, John was able to come up with a trait or characteristic for many of his classmates from personal knowledge or through conversations with close friends. However, there were some classmates who kept to themselves and remained relatively anonymous throughout their four years of dental school. They presented a real challenge when it came time to sketching their caricatures.

Now that I have hopefully piqued your curiosity, I will show you some of John's terrific artwork. I have six examples. First you will see the student's actual yearbook photo, followed by John's rendition of them.

You'll be amazed at the likeness of each classmate's yearbook photo with John's drawing of that person. I'll 'splain' the meaning of each as we go along. Just keep in mind … John did this over and over and over—79 times!

Let's start with Kevin Grace. Kevin, famous for his impressive handlebar mustache, was also Class President for their last three years of dental school.

Since some of our country's most famous Presidents—George Washington, Abraham Lincoln, Andrew Jackson—already had their portraits on the $1, $5 and $20 bills respectively, John gave Kevin his *own* denomination, the ever-popular $3 bill!

Jill Frier, a gal who wore her hair long, her skirts short and clogs, was known as a free-spirit.

John, recalling our 1967 camping trip when we had strolled around the Haight-Ashbury section of San Francisco, known for its hippie population, drew her like this:

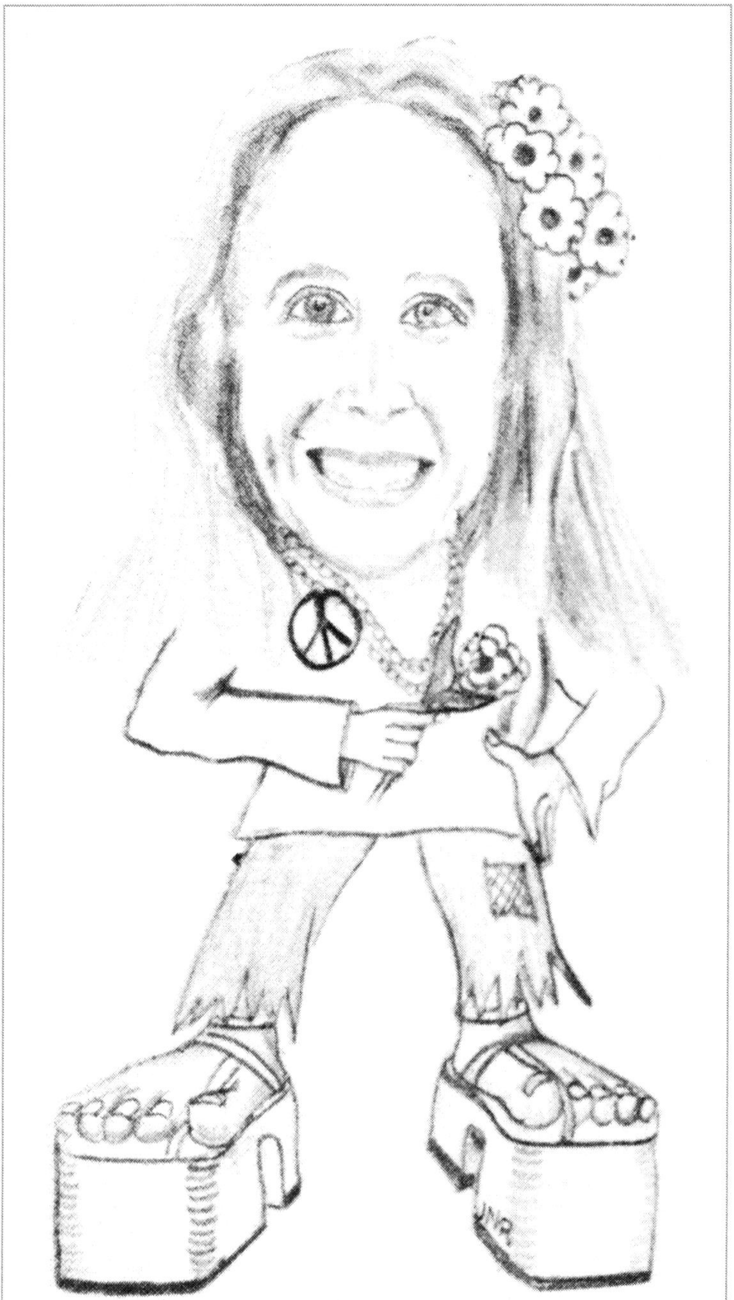
JNR

Another classmate, Doug Masi, was a physical fitness buff—lifting weights, jogging. A short fellow, he was really muscular and strong ... a powerhouse.

This is how John depicted him:

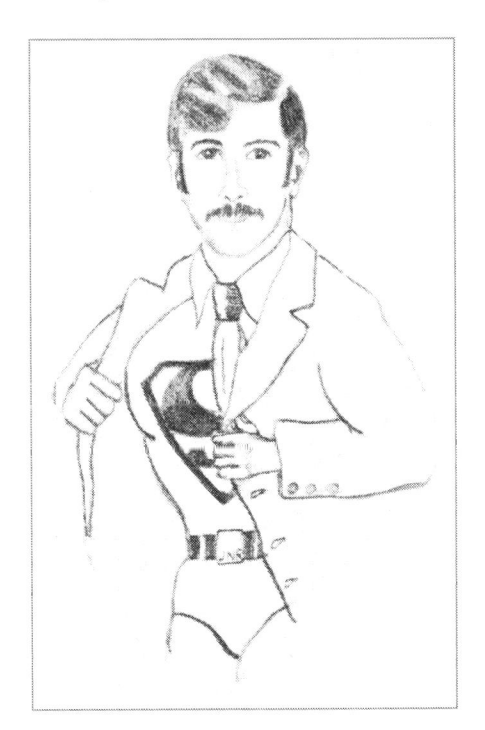

Brad Saisselin, from New England, was a huge fan of any professional sports team in Boston, be it the Red Sox, the Patriots, the Celtics, the Minutemen or the Bruins.

Fellow classmate Neil Eisler had quite a head of hair, which John used to his advantage:

And lastly, but hardly 'leastly', John drew himself.

This is John's yearbook photo. But in his self-portrait, he used a different photo of himself, taken from a different angle, because it was a better fit for his sketch.

Perhaps you are familiar with the portrait that the famous illustrator, Norman Rockwell, did of himself. Norman is seated on a stool in front of his easel, leaning to one side while looking in a mirror to see his reflection. John always thought that Norman's self-portrait was really clever, so he decided to employ the same idea for his own caricature.

Pretty good, huh?
As I have said in the past, John is one multi-talented fellow!

706 Suffern Road - 1978

At the beginning of his fourth and final year of dental school in 1977, John learned about a dental internship program being offered by the Air Force.

The one-year internship rotated each resident through various dental specialties under the tutelage of board-certified Air Force dentists in that particular specialty.

The specialties included were: endodontics (root canals), periodontics (gums), prosthodontics (crowns, bridges, implants, dentures), orthodontics (braces), pediatric dentistry (children), oral surgery (extractions, implants, trauma and corrective surgery), and oral pathology (oral disease).

Whew! Ain't that a mouthful! But then ... what else is dentistry if *not* a mouthful! The internship offered very beneficial post-doctoral training so John did not hesitate to apply.

At the time, the internship program was offered at ten different Air Force bases around the country. It was a highly-sought-after program and the competition was fierce.

Several months later, in early 1978, we learned that John *had* been accepted into the internship program and would receive his training at Keesler Air Force Base's Medical Center in Biloxi, Mississippi, situated right on the Gulf of Mexico.

Now knowing where we were going following John's graduation in May, it was time to start thinking about selling our house.

John did not like the idea of listing our house with a realtor and paying a real estate commission from whatever profit was made on the sale. He wanted us to try selling it ourselves. By eliminating the commission, we could price our home lower than comparable homes in our area and hopefully, sell it more quickly.

But we had no idea how to price our house. We had lived in it for almost four years and together had painted every single room. Additionally, John had made a number of structural improvements.

Since we had paid $46,000 for our home in 1974, we decided to price it at $56,000 based upon our highly deductive reasoning and well-thought-out strategy that if we could make $10,000 in four years, we would be thrilled!

We told some of our neighbors that we were going to try to sell our home ourselves and were about to put it on the market when, out of the blue, I got a phone call from Irene, a gal who lived on the street behind us.

I didn't know Irene but she told me that she was a realtor. She had heard through the grapevine that we were moving and intended to sell our home ourselves. Irene asked if she could see our home and assured me that there would be no strings attached.

I agreed and a few minutes later, she was on my doorstep, asking for a tour. She was very complimentary about our home's condition, the way it "showed" and the great improvements we had made. When the tour was over, she offered a proposal.

Irene said that she had a few clients who might be very interested in our house and she wanted to hold an Open House that coming weekend. She told me that she did *not* want us to sign a contract of any kind and that there would be no obligation on our part. She just wanted to show it on Saturday and Sunday and see what would happen.

Wanting to know what we were going to ask for our home, I told her our hoped-for figure of $56,000 and she was flabbergasted! Irene said that $56,000 was *too low*, that she would price it at $63,900. Well, I almost fell over! She said that if she sold it, she would then draw up a contract, but if there was no sale, we were free to pursue selling it on our own.

As far as I was concerned, this was a win-win situation. We had nothing to lose and everything to gain. After conferring with John, we agreed to Irene's proposal.

Irene had four couples go through our Open House that Saturday. She told us later that one couple in particular, the Thompkins, had spent a long time in each room, asking many questions.

On Sunday, another three couples went through our house and the Thompkins returned for another look, a very good sign.

Irene called us on Sunday evening saying that the Thompkins wanted to buy our house for $63,900 and they were ready to seal the deal with a contract.

Needless-to-say, we were speechless and overjoyed. The Thompkins wanted to move in at the same time we were planning to move out so everything came together perfectly.

I have never forgotten Irene and we gladly paid the commission.

Now for the kicker:

If you recall, our house had 3 upstairs bedrooms and the den John had created. The only bathroom was upstairs and there was an unheated, glass-enclosed back porch.

We had become very good friends with our immediate next-door neighbors during our four years on Suffern Road. Marie and Lou Szalay were a wonderful retired couple. Through letters, I kept in touch with the Szalays for years after we moved. Marie kept us informed of the 'goings-on' in our old neighborhood and they became good friends with the Thompkins as well.

We moved to Biloxi in June 1978 and the Thompkins moved in, right behind us.

In 1980, Marie wrote that the Thompkins had had some major work done on our former home. They'd had heating installed on the back porch and had a half-bath built out there, too.

In 1983, five years after we sold our Teaneck home for $63,900, New Jersey was in the midst of a white-hot, booming real estate market. The Thompkins were moving out of state and had put our old home on the market, listing it as a 3-bedroom home **with den, a heated back porch and 1 ½ bathrooms.**

They sold it in one day.

If you recall, not only was the house convenient to Fairleigh Dickinson University, it was one block from an entrance ramp onto Route 4, a major highway that went directly to the George Washington Bridge and New York City. As they say in real estate … Location, Location, Location.

Remember that we had bought the house for $46,000, lived in it for four years, and sold it for $63,900. The Thompkins upgraded the back porch, lived in the house for 5 years, and sold it for … are you *ready* for this? … $209,000!!!!!!

WAAAH!!Wah-Wah-WAAAAAH!!!!

☙❧

Keesler Air Force Base - 1978

John graduated from Fairleigh Dickenson with a DMD in May 1978, a wonderful day in the Rogerson household!

At first, I couldn't get over the fact that he would now be called Doctor Rogerson. I never would have imagined that I was marrying a future dentist back in 1966. A *dentist?* Who he?

On the day he graduated, John was also promoted back to captain, the rank he had been four years earlier and for three years prior to that.

I threw a big graduation/celebration dinner party and invited family, friends and neighbors. Our local grocery store, Pathmark, copied my design and inscription perfectly on John's cake:

We sold our Plymouth Valiant and after loading our two daughters, Barney and our luggage into our big Dodge van, we drove to Keesler Air Force Base in Biloxi, Mississippi. As soon as we got on base, we went directly to the Housing Office to get our names placed on the base house waiting list.

As luck would have it, they had several empty, recently renovated homes available, all on the same block. We were told that we could pick any one of them and move in right away, that very day.

Since Barney was not allowed to stay with us in any temporary military lodging facility, we decided to sign on the dotted line and move into a completely empty house. We figured that all of our household goods were going to be delivered in a few short days anyway and surely we could 'camp out' in an empty house until then. It might actually be fun, an adventure!

Thank heavens we had our big Dodge van for hauling. We were able to borrow two rollaway cots, sleeping bags, pots and pans, utensils and sundry items from Family Services on base to tide us over. And since we needed new sheets, towels and pillows, I ran into the Base Exchange, bought those, then dashed to the commissary for groceries.

We moved into 451 Kensington Drive, our Keesler home, later that afternoon. It was a three bedroom, two bath ranch only 300 feet from what is called the Back Bay—a very large body of water that is actually part of the Gulf of Mexico. The Housing Office had informed us that our house was five feet below sea level. Below sea level? Hmmm…

We were also told that nine years earlier in 1969, when Hurricane Camille, a Category 5 hurricane, hit Biloxi and the Gulf Coast, our newly-assigned base house had filled with water reaching a mere foot from the ceiling! How convenient … a house *and* a swimming pool, all in one.

But we had been reassured that our home and the others nearby, with their recent renovations, were now practically brand new. We just hoped there would be no more hurricanes during our time at Keesler. HAH! No Such Luck!

That first evening in our house, we had a humdinger of a thunderstorm that knocked out the electricity. I didn't have candles or matches and all the other homes near us were unoccupied. We only had a flashlight from our van for light but thankfully, thirty minutes later, our power returned.

After the electricity came back on, I went into our kitchen for a glass of water and as I flipped on the switch for the overhead fluorescent light, I saw two 5-inch long antennae protruding from behind the switch-plate. **AAAIIIIEEE!** I screamed and John came running.

The antennae slowly retreated behind the switch-plate, which made my skin crawl. John got a screwdriver, unscrewed the switch-plate but the roach, or palmetto bug as the natives call them, was nowhere to be found. But if I'd had a saddle, I knew Betsy could have ridden him!

Jennifer and Betsy slept on their bedroom linoleum floor in sleeping bags, John and I slept on the rollaway cots in the master bedroom and Barney slept on the linoleum floor between us. So began our life in Mississippi.

It wasn't too bad at first and we certainly managed. However, after several days of 'making do' with poor lighting from dim overhead bulbs, living out of suitcases on the floor and with our only furniture consisting of a card table and 4 folding chairs, camping out got old very quickly. I got more and more anxious to have our household goods arrive.

A week later, when they hadn't, John called our moving company in Fenton, Missouri. He was told that our moving van was ... let's see ... oh yes, in western Ohio picking up a small shipment. The dispatcher assured us that we would hear soon about its arrival date.

Another week passed and still no moving van. John called again and this time the dispatcher said that our moving van was in ... let's see ... oh yes, in northern Michigan BUT we would hear from them very soon about delivery.

Another week passed ... then another.

Our moving van finally pulled up in front of our house five weeks after we had moved into our Keesler house ... **FIVE WEEKS!!!!!**

We got all kinds of lame excuses as to why it had taken so long but they had us over the proverbial 'barrel'. There had been nothing we could do about it.

"Dem's de breaks" the moving van driver said.

You gotta' learn to roll with the punches, especially when you're a military family and moves are frequent ... but five weeks?????

CR☙

Tillie the Twirler - 1979

Before I begin, I need to rewind for a minute.

In 1978, when we were still living in New Jersey and before we moved to Keesler Air Force Base, John and I had gone to an outdoor concert featuring Karen and Richard Carpenter at the Garden State Performing Arts Center in Holmdel, New Jersey.

Their lead-in act was none other than Neil Sedaka. He had been out of the spotlight for a few years and was on a comeback tour. Neil had great rapport with the audience and was a terrific entertainer. He sang some of his biggest hits—"Breakin' Up is Hard to Do", "Happy Birthday, Sweet Sixteen" and "Calendar Girl". Buying Neil's album "All You Need Is the Music" sometime later, there was a song on it that we had not heard before. Titled "Tillie the Twirler", it was written by Neil Sedaka and Howard Greenfield.

Now fast-forward to Keesler AFB.

In the spring of 1979, the Keesler Officers Club was going to host a dinner party followed by some unique entertainment. After dinner, they were going to have a Beauty Pageant. There would be ten contestants and three judges. Each contestant would parade across the stage appropriately attired and would be asked questions by the Master of Ceremonies, our base commander, Colonel Amdall. A grand prize would be awarded to the winner.

This was called "The $1.98 Beauty Pageant" but this was not going to be an ordinary beauty pageant. Oh no, there was a twist. All of the beauty contestants were going to be *men*, various officers from around the base, and John was asked to be one of them. John readily agreed but that evening when he told me about it, we wondered what kind of costume he could wear. How could we dress John up to look like a beauty contestant?

I suddenly remembered Neil's album. I dug it out and finding the song about "Tillie the Twirler", I listened to it carefully:

> ♪ Down at the Bijou they stand in line, ♪
> The movie's lousy but the show's real fine.
> They got a gal there you won't forget,
> She's got the power of an old prop jet.

> When she's on the stage she always gives you her all,
> If you know your geography then you'll recall -
> Minneapolis and Saint Paul,
> When Tillie twirls her tassels around.

Gee, could John to go as the fictitious Tillie? We had two tassels from school graduation mortarboards in our props suitcase and I had that long-haired brown wig that you saw Barney wearing earlier. Tassels and a wig weren't much but they were a start.

> You see she wants to be a prima ballerina,
> So tell me everybody doesn't that redeem her?
> She's got to make a living,
> To pay for all those lessons
>
> Won't you let this stripper
> Trade a G-string for a slipper.
> She's the next Pavlova, So won't you think it over.
> Let Tillie twirl her tassels around.

John went shopping and bought a pair of extra-large black nylon undies, black fishnet stockings, platform sneakers and the biggest black bra he could find ... 46 DD!

Wanting to model his outfit for me, John put everything on when he got home. He stuffed his bra with rolled up athletic socks ... LOTS of socks! When he emerged from our bedroom as Tillie, I laughed so hard I almost wet my pants! With a little make-up and a few additional touches, we completed his 'Tillie look'. We were ready for the party.

We went to the party in regular party clothes but once the 'beauty contestants' had eaten, we were given the heads-up to go into a back room to prepare for the pageant.

One fellow, a pilot, plopped a frosted wig on his head and changed into a mid-thigh length white skirt, a bra and a white V-neck t-shirt. Swinging a tennis racket with one hand, he pulled tennis balls out of his bra and hit them out, into the audience! He was Renee Richards, the transgender professional tennis player. He made quite an impression, but me-oh-my, what hairy legs!

One of our chaplains dressed as Dolly Parton. He covered his balding head with a bouffant blonde wig and slipped into his wife's nightgown. Two large balloons enhanced the nightgown while an inch of pancake makeup covered his five o-clock stubble nicely. For Air Force friends of ours who may remember, this was Chaplain Art Homer. His wife, Sharon, helped get him into his 'get up".

With my help, John dressed as Tillie. As I drew a beauty spot high on John's cheekbone with a black marker and applied lipstick, he unwrapped several pieces of bubble gum and started chewing. He was told that he would be contestant #10, the last one to be called out from the wings.

I rushed back into the dining room so I could watch the entire pageant. I didn't want to miss a second of it.

When the first 'beauty' made her entrance, you knew that the show was going to be a smashing success. The men played their roles to the hilt and each 'gal' was dressed funnier than the last. The men out in the audience were catcalling and wolf whistling like mad. It was hysterical!

Colonel Amdall asked silly questions of each contestant and each gave very funny answers.

Finally, it was John's turn. He sashayed out on stage chewing his wad of gum like a cow chewing her cud and the audience went wild! Colonel Amdall asked him to introduce himself.

In the best Brooklyn accent he could muster and in a high voice, John squeaked, "I'm Tillie the Twoilah from Noo Yawk City. Pleased ta' make ya' acquaintance." Tillie then brushed her hair away from her face and shimmied her shoulders.

Colonel Amdall, doubled over laughing, asked Tillie if she could really twirl her tassels.

"Sure, Hon." Tillie replied. "Let me give youse a demo."

Taking a step back, Tillie assumed an appropriate pose and twirled those tassels so fast she almost propelled herself off the ground! To further demonstrate her artistry, she then twirled them in the opposite direction. I tell you, that Tillie had talent! The audience screamed with delight!

> Let Tillie twirl her tassels,
> Don't give her any hassles -
> Let Tillie twirl her tassels around!

To impress the judges further, Tillie left the stage to greet each one "up close and personal"—one of whom was Colonel Rusty Sloan, the hospital commander and John's ultimate boss.

Tossing her hair around like Tina Turner, Tillie strutted down the front stairs and off the stage. With mincing steps, she walked over to the judges' table and, calling each "Sweetheart", she sat down on each of their laps. Patting them on their heads and using her sultry voice, she purred, "Why don't you come up and see me sometime!"

Swiveling her hips to the max as she minced back to the stage, Tillie proceeded to blow kisses to everyone in the audience. The roar of laughter was deafening and Colonel Sloan was laughing so hard, I thought he was going to split his sides!

Tillie had one final interview question to answer. Chewing her massive wad of gum, she flirtatiously tossed her hair away from her face as she listened to the question. Opening her mouth to answer, a strand of hair got caught in her mouth and the gum wad immediately stuck to it. During a dramatic moment in Tillie's impassioned plea for "world peace", the highly visible wad of gum, now attached to her hair, flew out of her mouth and swung like a pendulum next to her face.

Without missing a beat, Tillie tossed her gorgeous locks with perfect speed and timing so that when she opened her mouth again, she caught the wad between her teeth on the fly. A refined "Lady of the Evening", Tillie gently pulled the strands of hair from her mouth while continuing to enjoy her chewing gum. Tillie maintained her poise and composure throughout the entire incident and was awarded with a standing ovation! I tell you ... What a gal! What class!

Needless-to-say, Tillie won the "$1.98 Beauty Pageant" and became a Legend in Her Own Mind!

She was presented with a bottle of vintage 1979 champagne approximately two months old, a wilted bouquet of flowers, a trophy and a massive cardboard check in the amount of ... you guessed it, $1.98. I was so proud! It was an evening never to be forgotten!

I had Tillie put her outfit on again the next day so I could take her picture on our front porch. I knew her celebrity status would spread far and wide and I wanted to capture Tillie with her winnings before she was overwhelmed with paparazzi.

There was no doubt, Tillie had taken the Officers Club by storm.

When you see Tillie's picture, be sure to notice Barney looking at Tillie through our screen door. Even he is laughing!

Please note, too, that Tillie had paid tribute to the Air Force with her belly-button 'tattoo' – I love (heart) the Air Force.

Also notice the dollar bill tucked in Tillie's black undies. This was a tip one of the judges had slipped into her waistband during the contest. The judge was obviously a true 'patron of the arts!'

You can see just how proud she is of having won such a prestigious contest and before such an esteemed audience. She was thrilled.

Believe me, no one can "strut her stuff" like Tillie can … and did!

Alas, it is with sadness that I have to report that Tillie never did achieve her goal of becoming a ballerina. But her newfound notoriety had folks clamoring for her appearance at every base to which we were assigned after Keesler.

And so, without further ado -

LAAAAAADIES AND GENTLEMEN

Let me introduce you to …

The ONE, … The ONLY

The Incomparable

"FIRST LADY OF THE AIR FORCE"

Heeeeeeeeere she is …

TILLIE THE TWIRLER!!

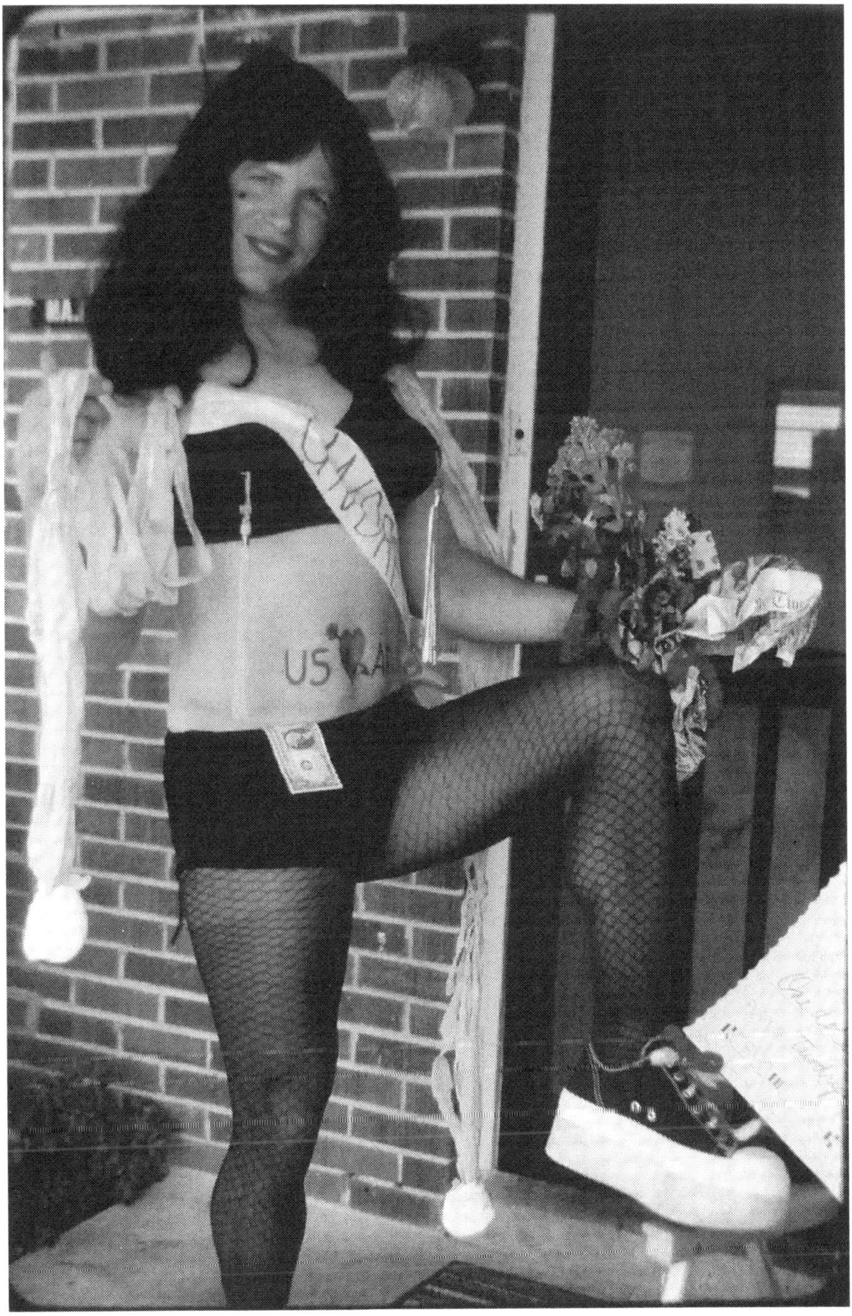
US

Hurricane Frederic

In the spring of 1979, we expected to leave Keesler that summer. John was in the last of his dental specialty rotations when he came to the realization that out of all the specialties in which he had received training, he enjoyed prosthodontics the most. He liked the variety of work that it involved and the varied technical and artistic skills it demanded.

A board-certified Air Force prosthodontist, Dr. (Col.) Anthony DiBello—who had instructed John during his internship at Keesler—recommended that John apply for the three-year Prosthodontics Residency Program offered by the Air Force. It entailed a year of academic instruction and the completion of a master's thesis at the University of Texas Graduate School of Dentistry in Houston, Texas.

Following this, if selected for the program, John would be sent to Wilford Hall Hospital at Lackland AFB for the following two years to undergo intensive clinical training. Wilford Hall is the Air Force equivalent of the Navy's Bethesda and the Army's Walter Reed hospitals.

John explained prosthodontics to me as a dental specialty involving diagnoses and treatment planning, designing and making crowns, bridges, partial dentures, full dentures and implants, and working with the latest in dental materials. It all sounded exciting ... to John. Dr. DiBello further advised John that with his extensive training, he would be much more valuable to the Air Force and that it could enhance his career.

John applied and with strong recommendations, he was accepted into the program, which meant he would have another three years as a student! Because the program had already accepted their residents for the class beginning in the summer of 1979, John spent a second year at Keesler as a general dentist, awaiting the start of his residency class in the summer of 1980. The girls and I settled in for another year at the base.

Jennifer and Betsy, in 4th and 2nd grade respectively, were bused to Gorenflo Elementary School off base. The school did something every day of the school year that I found unique. Jennifer and Betsy's classes stopped for a "Goober Break" in the afternoon. Small, white disposable cups, the kind hospitals use to dispense pills, were filled with peanuts and passed out to each student. I guess it was a nutritious, inexpensive way to give the kids a little energy boost ... a Goober Break. I'm glad it wasn't a Booger Break!

However, what gave me pause during that summer of 1979, was something I had never seen before, something that our commissary (grocery store) did.

Beginning June 1st, the official start of the hurricane season, the commissary's paper grocery bags were printed with a grid of the Gulf of Mexico so that you could, if necessary, plot the coordinates of an approaching hurricane. Well, wasn't that handy, I thought. And then, darn it all, one day in early September, I needed to start plotting.

Hurricane Frederic, having just entered the Gulf of Mexico, was strengthening. As always with hurricanes, no one knew exactly where it was headed, but it kept on a-coming northward, churning away, inching closer and closer to the Mississippi Gulf Coast.

Remember now that our house was 5-feet below sea level. Local news out of New Orleans started broadcasting dire warnings of the potential damage a storm like Frederic could produce and advised us how to prepare for the worst. TV programs constantly aired the footage of the utter devastation left behind when Hurricane Camille came through the area in 1969 – ten years earlier.

September 12th, around 6 a.m., we knew we were in for it. Frederic's winds were over 100 mph, the storm was going to strengthen throughout the day, and it was predicted to make landfall somewhere along the Gulf Coast of Mississippi or Alabama later that night. Biloxi and Keesler Air Force Base might be directly in its path.

All the schools in Biloxi closed. John went to the dental clinic at 7:30 a.m. only to be told that the base was officially closed. When he got back home, I went outside to greet him and noticed something neither of us had ever seen before.

Even though it was still partly sunny, the outer bands of the approaching hurricane were now above us. These clouds had patterns in white concentric arcs, like a section of an enormous bulls-eye over the Back Bay and southern Mississippi—chilling, to say the least.

John and I started inverting chairs and other furniture on tabletops, counter tops, and beds, anywhere to get things off the floor. John grabbed photo albums, our strongbox, my jewelry box and other valued possessions we could think of and put them all in our van.

By 10 a.m., it was completely overcast and the wind was picking up. Military trucks, manned by Air Force security police, began rumbling up and down our streets using a bullhorn to announce that our entire neighborhood was under a **MANDATORY EVACUATION**. Other security personnel jumped out of the trucks and started sandbagging both our front and side doors.

We were instructed to go to our designated evacuation shelter, the basement of our base hospital. No pets of any kind were allowed in any of the evacuation shelters and we were told to leave them in our homes or release them outdoors to fend for themselves.

I beg your pardon. There was no way on God's green earth I was going to leave Barney in our house or abandon him. My mind was reeling.

I thought of the Biloxi lighthouse on the beach a few hundred feet in from the Gulf of Mexico. It is one of Biloxi's most prominent landmarks. Made of cast iron, it had been built in 1848 ... **1848!!!** ... and had withstood many hurricanes in its 131-year history, even Hurricane Camille with her sustained winds over 150mph ... and gusts to 200mph!

I figured, if necessary, I could lash Barney and myself together around that lighthouse (away from the Gulf side, of course) reasoning that if the lighthouse had survived such repeatedly violent weather, maybe we would, too. In retrospect, we probably would have found it easier to just strap ourselves to a toilet in our house since that was often one of the only fixtures remaining intact when a house was lifted off its foundation!

Fortunately, I didn't have to take either of those actions.

Steve Landin, a dentist John worked with, and his wife Cindy were a young couple and we often played bridge together. They lived on the other side of the flight line from our home and since their base house was on higher ground, they did not have to evacuate.

When the Landins heard that our housing area was under mandatory evacuation, they phoned and invited us, with Barney, to their house to spend the night. Not having any children of their own yet, it was very kind of them to take us in.

Before leaving home, I made all of us an early lunch. While the girls gathered their games, books and a few toys, John and I packed flashlights, batteries, candles, matches, a transistor radio, a couple of suitcases, sleeping bags, pillows and various food items. I emptied my freezer and refrigerator of as much food as possible, we grabbed

Barney's leash, bowls and food and drove to the Landins. That was at 1 p.m. and it had just started raining.

By 3 p.m., the rain was coming down hard and the wind was blowing it sideways. By 5:30 p.m., it was pitch black outside and then pitch black inside as the power went out.

With no power, I made everyone peanut butter and jelly sandwiches for dinner. The girls were content playing with their toys. Barney lay under the Landin's dining room table while we adults listened to storm reports on our transistor radio.

By 9 p.m., the wind was so strong and deafening that we had to shout to be heard. We put the girls in their sleeping bags and they promptly fell asleep. Tornadoes were being reported in various counties near us and by 10 p.m., we could hear the gutters and shingles being ripped off the Landin's roof. The wind picked up pebbles from the street and pelted the windows like gunshot.

At one point, I opened the blinds just a little to peek outside. Trees were being shaken violently from one side to the other by the howling wind. It was terrifying. Around midnight, tornadoes were all around us and we prepared for the worst. Suddenly and without warning, the heavy 3'x3' attic access lid in the hallway ceiling was sucked up into the attic only to come crashing down onto the hallway floor. It immediately woke the girls up and made them cry.

We ran into the hallway with our flashlights and saw the attic access wide open with pink insulation dropping to the floor. The constant creaking of the house, the deafening roar of the wind, the pounding rain and the sound of the gutters and downspouts slamming against the exterior brick walls made us wonder if we were about to experience the sound of an approaching freight train— a sound often associated with a tornado. Fortunately we never did.

An hour later, even though the others stayed up, I went to bed and managed to fall to sleep. I woke up just after 6 a.m. to find it was light outside ... and very quiet. The sun was coming out. The storm had passed.

We opened the blinds and saw the Landin's gutters hanging in shreds down over their windows. Shingles, tree branches, leaves and other debris was everywhere. The power was still out.

Listening again to our transistor radios, we learned that Hurricane Frederic had winds clocked at 125mph. We had received over ten inches of rain and the tides were estimated to have been eight to twelve feet above normal. Oh brother.

We were very anxious to get back to our own home to see what condition it was in, so after a quick breakfast, we loaded up our family and belongings, thanked the Landins and drove home.

As we approached our neighborhood, we were shocked to see the destruction of hundreds of trees blown over and lying on the ground with their tops pointing north, away from the Gulf.

Cars left out on the streets or in driveways had paid the price as virtually every window had been 'shot out' by the pebbles and stones picked up by the wind. It looked like the work of the Chicago Valentine's Day massacre!

We pulled into our driveway ... and everything looked okay. We opened our side door and thankfully, no gushing water poured out. Except for three windows in the front of our house that had leaked around the windowsills, everything was dry, intact, undamaged. We breathed a huge sigh of relief. However, we did not have power for the next five days.

The heat and humidity of September returned with a vengeance and it was all we could do to just survive in our sweltering house. People were throwing away whole freezers full of thawing, spoiling food.

The whine of chainsaws filled the air constantly as work crews cut up the toppled trees and hauled them away.

We learned that 500,000 people had been evacuated from the Gulf Coast in anticipation of Frederic's arrival. In its wake, there was an estimated $2.3 BILLION in damages.

Because of that extensive destruction, the name Frederic was retired and will never again be used in naming a hurricane.

And guess what? After the storm passed, the Biloxi lighthouse was still standing. Barney and I would probably have gotten a 'wee bit wet', but we would have been okay.

I hope I never have to go through an experience like that again ... ever. We were very fortunate.

ಙೞ

♪ *"We're in the Money"* ♪

Sometime in early 1979, John received a letter saying that a lawsuit was going to be filed against the Air Force by men and women in the Air Force who had been demoted to 2nd lieutenant during their years in either medical, dental or law school. There was a rumor going around that the other military services had NOT demoted their personnel during their schooling.

John was asked to join the lawsuit but he did not want to get involved. He had agreed to being demoted back in 1974 and we had accepted that requirement. We were just so pleased to have John's schooling paid for while he was drawing a salary.

Months later, we learned that the rumor was true. The Army, Navy and the Marines had not demoted their personnel as a condition for accepting their military sponsorship. They had maintained their existing rank, had never had their pay reduced and never had to buy "Day-Old" bread!

Well, how unfair is that!

Ultimately, a general from the Air Force Personnel Office wrote a letter to John and all similarly affected Air Force officers, inviting them to apply for a Change of Military Record. John supplied the necessary documents and in time, restoration of his rank, salary and "time in grade" were instituted and reflected in his military record. It was assumed that the Air Force realized they had been in error.

Some months later and out of the blue, John got a check in the mail for $12,000. I repeat … **$12,000!!!** The money represented all of John's back pay as if he had gone through dental school as a captain.

Holy Cow, what a windfall! We felt like we had just won the Publishers Clearing House Sweepstakes! We immediately deposited the money in our savings account.

A few weeks after that, John's "time in grade" of captain meant that he was now eligible for promotion to major. Along with his new promotion came a nice pay hike. We thought we had hit the jackpot! We could not believe our good fortune.

Our newfound wealth was not burning a hole in our pockets, but there was something we definitely needed to buy. John was riding his

Honda motor scooter to the dental clinic every day but it was becoming increasingly clear that we needed a second car, especially on days when it poured.

John has always loved Mercedes Benz cars and had always wanted one. I suggested that perhaps this was the perfect opportunity for him to buy his dream car.

We drove back to New Jersey that December in our big Dodge van to spend the Christmas holidays with our families. My parents lived in Closter, not too far from Benzel-Busch, the Mercedes Benz dealership in Englewood. While visiting my mother and father, we decided to pay the dealership a visit. We wanted to see what Mercedes models they had, learn a little more about them and check out prices.

On our way to the dealership, I giddily chirped to John how we might *never* have an unexpected $12,000 fall into our laps again and we should take advantage of this golden opportunity. I told John that he could pick out *whichever* Mercedes he wanted. With $12,000 in our pockets, **THE SKY WAS THE LIMIT!!!**

I thought, *What a wonderful, ever-thoughtful, selfless wife I am. John is **such** a lucky guy.*

A well-dressed salesman greeted us as we walked through the front door of Benzel-Busch. The elegant showroom sparkled with beautiful, highly polished Mercedes automobiles and classical music played quietly in the background.

But oh my goodness ... what was this? Every model in their showroom was higher priced than the next ... and they started at $22,000! It took the wind right out of our sails. Suddenly The Sky, which had been SO HIGH, was at ground level.

We finally asked the salesman to show us the *least-expensive* model they had in stock.

He took us outside to their parking lot and showed us a brand-new, just-delivered 1980 China blue 240D ("D" for diesel) model. It was a 4-cylinder, 4-door sedan with chrome bumpers, chrome hubcaps, chrome trim on the doors and trunk and of course, the three-pronged chrome Mercedes hood ornament above that famous chrome grill. The interior was dark blue.

For John it was love at first sight!

We asked the price. It was $17,000. WHAT? This was their least expensive new car and it was SEVENTEEN THOUSAND DOLLARS??? We remembered buying our brand-new, four-door

Plymouth Valiant ten years earlier for $2,500. Now we were looking at a car in a whooole 'nother category.

But, we both liked the China blue color and John did have his heart set on buying a Mercedes. My ability to rationalize kicked in as I pointed out that we would ***never*** be able to buy a brand-new Mercedes again with only a $5,000 out-of-pocket expense. **WHAT A BARGAIN!!!** We bought it then and there!

We now had two vehicles to drive the 1,275 miles back to Mississippi, our Dodge van and the new Mercedes. What were we thinking? We decided to take turns driving the new car and John wanted me to drive it first.

John led the way with Jennifer, Betsy and Barney in the van while I followed in the Mercedes on the miserable Pennsylvania Turnpike. I was so nervous driving that expensive automobile that my nerves rattled whenever I moved the steering wheel.

Thankfully, the drive was fine and there were no mishaps but I tell you, the more I drove that Mercedes, the more aware I became of "Buyer's Remorse."

When I stopped at a traffic light, that diesel engine vibrated so much that I thought my teeth would jar loose.

The diesel engine was so loud, I had to blast the radio to hear it.

Finding a gas station that sold diesel gasoline was, on occasion, a real challenge.

One of the car's most endearing qualities was its pick up. Going down a steep hill with a strong tailwind and with my right foot depressing "the pedal to the metal", our new Mercedes was able to accelerate from 0 to 60mph in ten minutes!

Honestly, talk about 'depressing'. While it was a very safe, solid car, I felt like I was driving a Sherman tank. The only pick-up that car had … was John!

We had that Mercedes from 1980 to 2002, twenty-two years. When we sold it, it had 157,000 miles on the odometer, yet John was still reluctant to let it go. He kept telling me that a Mercedes diesel could go three times that far—more than half a million miles without any trouble—to the moon and back.

Oh yeah? Oddly enough, that is exactly what I had wanted to do to that car … send it to the Moon! But please, do NOT send it back!

♪ *"The Stars at Night, are Big and Bright* ♪

The summer of 1980 arrived and it was time to move to Houston. Contacting various dental colleagues who had already completed their residency-training program in Houston, we learned about homes that they had rented and we found one that met our needs.

Sight unseen, we rented a house at 7119 Osage in Sharpstown, a western suburb of Houston. The house had a completely fenced-in backyard, which was good for Barney, and it was within walking distance of the elementary school, good for Jennifer and Betsy.

We moved into the house on Friday, the 4th of July.

What we hadn't known was that no one had lived in the house for over six weeks, since the middle of May. The electricity had been turned off in May and no one had done a lick of yard work. Added to that, we were also moving into a Texas heat wave of epic proportions.

As we pulled into the driveway of our new rental home, the front yard was completely overgrown. The backyard looked like The Great Plains with grass three feet high. Over the next few days Barney, naturally, did his 'business' in the backyard. When I went out to scoop up his messes, I felt like I was tramping through a minefield! One false step and eeeUUU!

Upon arriving at our rental home, we also found the moving truck waiting for us. Walking up to the house, we opened the front door and a blast of hot air almost knocked us over. Because the power had been turned off, there was no air-conditioning. A plastic thermometer propped up on the kitchen windowsill read 115 degrees. Opening windows and the sliding glass doors didn't help because it was 112 degrees outside!

A call to the utility company brought bad news. The dispatcher was sorry but because it was a holiday, there would be no service hook-up until Monday morning at the *earliest*. We had to live without power for three whole days. We couldn't turn any lights on. I couldn't put any food in the refrigerator. We couldn't turn ceiling fans on or use the electric stove.

Our household goods were offloaded in record time. I didn't blame the movers. They wanted to get out of our hothouse and back into their air-conditioned truck as quickly as possible.

Thinking about our situation, our over-riding concern was about our beloved 11-year-old Barney in his heavy fur coat. He was panting a lot and kept searching for any cool spot.

John called the utility company again and explained our situation. The dispatcher was sympathetic and said that if we were willing to pay a $150 service charge, he would send someone out right away to turn the electricity back on. We were never so happy to fork over $150.

According to Wikipedia, the Texas heat wave of 1980 was a devastating natural disaster of intense heat and drought. The agricultural damage alone totaled $20 BILLION!

There were many consecutive days of triple-digit temperatures that broke many existing records. Wichita Falls, in the northern part of the state near the Oklahoma border, had recorded a temperature of 117 degrees in late June. Despite the heat, once we had air-conditioning, we were fine.

We settled into life in Houston and found the city an exciting place in which to live. Texas was "hot" in more ways than one in 1980.

The movie "Urban Cowboy" with John Travolta and Debra Winger was a smash hit. Gilley's bar, with its mechanical bull, was all the rage. Texas real estate was selling like hot cakes and there was no doubt, Texas was *the* place to be!

In mid-July, the Republican Convention was held in Detroit, Michigan. The Convention nominated Ronald Reagan as their presidential candidate and he chose George H.W. Bush as his running mate.

A few days later, Mr. Reagan and Mr. Bush made their first official appearance together in Houston, the Bushes' hometown. It was held at the Galleria, a beautiful mall. Houston was all abuzz and we wanted to see the candidates as well.

A band was playing amidst a dazzling display of banners, balloons, REAGAN-BUSH placards, American and Texas flags everywhere and wall-to-wall onlookers. We found a little space along the railing on the 3rd floor of the Galleria where we could look down and see a small stage that had been built on the 1st floor.

It was a thrill to see Mr. Reagan and Mr. Bush addressing the huge audience and when they were elected President and Vice-President respectively, that memory became even more special for us.

We also became fans of the Houston Oilers. Coach Bum Phillips, quarterback Ken Stabler and the running back, Earl Campbell, were all familiar names. We followed the team and watched their games on television every weekend.

For some inexplicable reason though, John also became a *big* fan of the Houston Oiler cheerleaders ... a really, *really* big fan! John was often preoccupied during the televised game writing up hypothetical treatment plans for his thesis, paying little attention to the football action on the TV screen.

HOWEVER, any time a TV cameraman happened to pan over to the Oiler cheerleaders—those scantily-clad, go-go booted, buxom, statuesque gals, shaking their boo ... I mean their pom-poms—John's head popped up like a submerged cork! He would sit and stare, completely mesmerized, while I blotted drool from his chin.

One morning we learned that the Oiler cheerleaders would be making a 5 p.m. appearance in a mall near Sharpstown that afternoon. Even though he was a *terribly overworked* resident with an *incredibly busy* schedule and a *full day* of classes, somehow John was able to rearrange his schedule so that the four of us could go see them.

All decked out in their white go-go boots and skimpy, red-white-and-blue patriotic cheerleading outfits, the Oiler cheerleaders had assembled in the courtyard of the mall. An enthusiastic crowd gathered and applauded as the gals did a few cheers and shook their pom-poms. I had no idea that John could wolf-whistle and hoot-n-holler at the same time!!

At the conclusion of their program, they offered to sign autographs. I had observed John eyeing a particularly endowed "bodacious blonde" but he was too embarrassed to ask "Bubbles" for her autograph. He sent Jennifer instead!

Do you remember when John had drawn all of his classmates' faces with caricature bodies for his *Dentoscope* yearbook back when he was in dental school? (See *Dentoscope*)

Well, for my 37th birthday in January 1981, John surprised me with a homemade birthday card. He used my head from an earlier, 1974 family photo as his model:

Ah yes, I was thirty-years old when this picture was taken and don't you just love the glasses? And look at my dark hair!

When my birthday rolled around and I opened his card, needless to say, I was bowled-over, speechless and extremely flattered.

On the outside of the card, John had written:

Give me a "T"
Give me an "E"
Give me an "A"
Give me an "M"!

Then I opened the card.
What do you think? Is this me or *WHAT??*

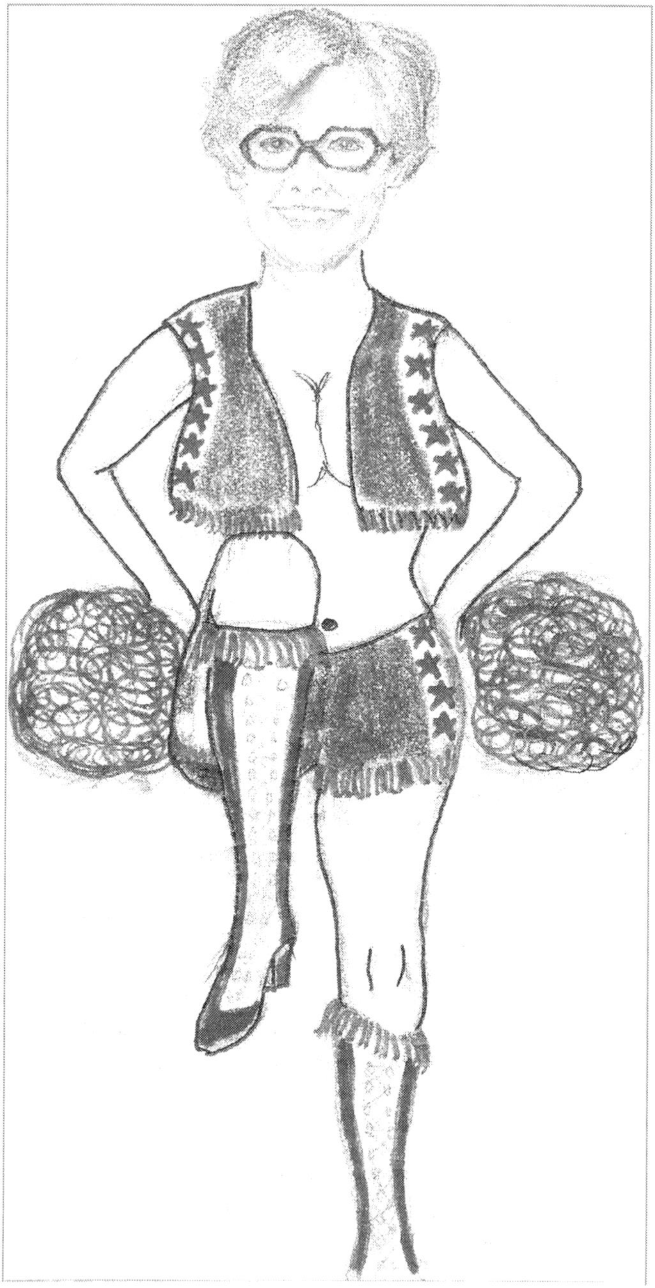

♫ *"What Goes Up, Must Come Down"* ♫

In 1981, four months before we were to move to San Antonio, we learned that several of John's dental colleagues, who were also moving to San Antonio to complete their residency training, had decided to have homes built in a residential section of the city called The Great Northwest.

We looked into it as well and were pleased with what we learned. We knew that we might not ever have the chance again to have a home built 'from scratch'.

Getting in touch with a builder and making numerous trips to San Antonio to work out the particulars, we had blueprints drawn up to John's design and specifications. Our new home would be a 2,500-sq.-ft., five-bedroom, 2½-bathroom house built on a pie-shaped lot at the end of a cul-de-sac that we had chosen. The address would be 8406 Timber Crown in the Silver Creek section of the Great Northwest Community and the house would cost $90,000.

WHAT??? In only seven years we were about to pay almost twice as much as we had for our first home in Teaneck? I cringed at the thought of having to pay so much.

Before we moved into our rental home in Houston, we had never lived in a home with ceiling fans, and we loved them. They kept the air circulating nicely and cooled down a room without having to lower the air-conditioner.

About a week after ordering our San Antonio home, I saw an ad in the *Houston Chronicle*, which caught my eye. A store was having a huge sale on Casablanca ceiling fans. Knowing that we were going to buy and install fans in our San Antonio home, we decided to take advantage of this sale and bought a fan for our future living room.

After buying the fan, John (who you remember is very handy) wanted to be sure it worked before we moved 200 miles away from the store where we bought it.

After assembling the new fan, John got out our six-foot stepladder and climbing it, took down the existing living room ceiling fan. Then with both of us up on the stepladder, I helped hold up the new fan while John screwed it to the escutcheon plate in the ceiling.

Taking the stepladder with him, John walked down a hallway and climbed up into the attic through the access panel. In order to get to the center of the living room to reinforce the support of the fan and to wire it in electrically, John had to walk along the top of the narrow 2x4 beams almost hidden by 18 inches of loose, blown-in pink insulation between each beam.

To give you the idea, picture John on a balance beam, carefully stepping from one beam to the other, all while cautiously weaving, dodging and stepping over a maze of air conditioning/heating ducts and ducking under roof trusses.

Waiting for John to reach the location of the fan, I sat down in the living room and resumed reading the newspaper. I could hear him overhead, the beams creaking and groaning, as he walked **EVER ... SOOO ... SLOOOWLY, STEP-BY-CAREFUL-STEP,** in my direction, heading for the center of the living room.

It was eerie, like having a ghost in the attic walking steadily and stealthily above my head.

A few seconds later, I heard a loud **THWACK!!**

"OUCH!"

"What happened?" I yelled, looking up.

"I'm okay," John replied, his voice muffled. He had smacked his head on one of the trusses.

He continued on with measured steps and was slowly approaching the center of the living room when—

CRASH!!!

John fell through the ceiling!

"AAAAAAAHHH!!!!"

I screamed as though I had been shot, and bolted out of the chair as ceiling plaster and pink insulation rained down into the living room and on my head.

I looked up to see John's two legs dangling above me! In falling, he had punched a huge hole in the living room ceiling. The falling debris reminded me of confetti in Times Square on New Year's Eve.

"**Good GRIEF!**" I shrieked. "Are you all right?"

"I'm okay, I'm okay." He was panting, not really sure if he was okay or not.

John was straddling a beam, which had kept him from falling all the way into the living room. Fortunately, when he felt himself begin to fall, he had locked his arms to brace himself and with his hands, he was able to stop from landing full force on the beam.

You cannot imagine what a "mell-of-a-hess" that shattered ceiling made with pieces of drywall of every size, chalky white dust and bits of pink insulation coating everything.

John lifted himself back up to a standing position. Concluding that the experience was not as much fun as he thought it would be, he decided that he wanted to avoid a repeat performance. He lay down across several beams and pulled himself the rest of the way, to the middle of the living room.

Dusting myself off and hauling the stepladder back into the living room, I climbed up to the new fan and braced it so that John could reinforce the mounting and connect the electrical wiring in the attic.

Telling me where to find the breaker box and which breaker to throw to provide power to the switch-plate, I turned on the fan control. Lo and behold, the fan blades started turning. It worked!

Now John had to do everything in reverse as he disconnected the new fan and reattached the old one.

That completed, the fact remained that we had a gaping hole in the living room ceiling. "Houston, we have a problem."

John was able to patch a large piece of sheetrock, tape and float the seams (I asked what John had done and he used that word again—'float') and repaint the ceiling.

Other than a slight fading of the original ceiling paint, the touch-up paint that had been left in the garage matched fairly well.

In recalling this story, I can't help but think how fortunate it was that John was able to cushion his fall and straddle the beam without landing on it with full force.

Had that *not* been the case, John might very well be singing soprano in our "Village Voices" chorus today!

CR&J

Six-Pack Flabs

I have been fighting Six-Pack Flabs for most of my life. We've all heard the saying that a woman can never be "too thin". Well I'm here to tell you that I have never been close to that description and the concept of being too thin is hard for me to grasp.

Do you have the same problem that I do in trying to lose weight? Isn't it just the *most* frustrating thing? GADS!

It wasn't long after we were married in 1966 that I began putting on weight—a pound here, another pound there—but back then when I was young, I could take it off relatively easily. But no more.

The older I got, the harder it became to lose weight and my metabolism got slower and slower as well. Weight started attaching itself to my arms, my tummy and thighs like barnacles on a ship ... impossible to remove!

I have been on many diets over the years—self-imposed diets, the Egg Diet, the Grapefruit Diet, the Three-Day to a New You Diet!, the Set-Point Diet, The Zone, The Scarsdale, Atkins and Weight Watchers, to name a few.

I had gained weight during our two years at Keesler and once we moved to Houston, I had put on even more. Bad, bad, bad.

During the year we lived in Houston, I kept seeing the same commercial on TV, day after day after day.

> *"If you are serious about losing weight, call 222-2222.*
> *We'll help you lose weight and keep it off.*
> *Call us today and don't delay."*

About a month before John finished his coursework in Houston and with our impending move to San Antonio, I decided that I wanted to, no, make that I *had* to lose weight. I called 222-2222.

Yes, I wanted to join their weight-loss program that very day. All I had to do was go to their office, fill out paperwork, pay $199 and meet with one of their 'diet specialists' who would explain the program to me.

I had just over four weeks to lose weight so that a 'new me' would move to San Antonio. I beat a path to their door and found the place packed!

Once I signed in, I was taken into one of their exam rooms. A 'diet specialist' explained the program to me. I was put on a scale and handed a booklet that explained everything. I was told what I had to do, what I could eat and what I couldn't, what portions I could have and how to calculate them.

I was also told that I would have to fill out a chart listing everything that I ate every single day, that I had to weigh each portion and that I had to turn in the chart each time I went to their office.

Besides having to drink eight 8-ounce glasses of water a day, I had to report to their offices three times a week—to weigh in, turn in my eating chart and pick up a new one. I was also required to drink their special concoction containing potassium and electrolytes and told that I would have to drink it in front of one of their 'diet specialists' during each visit.

Having to drink 64 ounces (HALF A GALLON!) of water daily was pure torture. I felt like I was drowning! I became a prisoner in my own home because once that water hit my bladder, I spent the rest of the day doing just one thing. I "skipped to my *loo*"!

The diet was strict, limiting me to a 3-ounce chicken breast or a small 3-ounce, lean hamburger patty, a little salad and a few vegetables.

The procedure was always the same. Once you signed in at the check-in counter, your chart was placed in a basket outside one of three treatment rooms. You then sat in the busy waiting room until your name was called.

Once that happened, you were directed to one of the treatment rooms where a 'diet specialist' weighed you, collected your eating chart and had you drink the 'special concoction'. I went to their offices three times a week for four weeks and was seen by a different 'diet specialist' each time!

The place was always hopping with women of all ages, shapes and sizes who were trying to lose weight just like me.

My problem was that the more weight I lost, the more shaky and nauseous I felt. There were times when I was so hungry that I could have eaten one of my arms. However, I ate my meager portions, I drank the required ocean of water and I checked in three times a week.

You know what? That crazy diet worked! My weight started

dropping like a stone. I lost seven pounds the first week, five the second and another five the third week.

At the end of the fourth week, I went in for my final weigh-in and office visit.

I signed in at the check-in counter and sat down in the waiting area, following the normal procedure.

The place was its usual beehive of activity with women signing in, women walking out, women talking with new-found friends, comparing progress notes with fellow 'losers', phones ringing off the hook ... a regular Grand Central Station at rush hour. It was very noisy.

I hadn't waited too long when door #3 opened and a client walked out, followed by yet another unfamiliar diet specialist. She grabbed the next chart in her basket and called out "Rogerson". I stood up and followed her into the treatment room.

Without saying a word she motioned for me to stand on the scale and she weighed me. Then mixing up the special concoction, she had me drink it.

We stood there as she started flipping through the pages in my chart, which looked unusually thick.

She looked over at me, scrunched up her face and asked, "How are you teeth?"

My teeth? Why is she asking about my teeth? I told her that they were fine.

She continued flipping through my chart pages, which prompted another question. "How's your back, still giving you problems?"

My back? Good grief! What's going on here?

I told her that my back was fine, that I had never had any problems with my back.

She looked at me quizzically. Flipping my chart to the registration form in front, she said, "You are Wanda, aren't you? Wanda Rogerson?"

HUH?

"No!" I replied, taken aback. "I'm Sherri. Sherri Rogerson. I'm not Wanda."

"Wait a minute", she went on, looking at my registration form more closely. "Isn't your husband Ernest?"

I paused, then said, "Sometimes," with a little grin.

I had lost another five pounds in my final week, a total of 22 pounds in four weeks.

As you have probably guessed, it was a temporary weight loss.

Most military moves, all moves really, are stressful to some degree and ours to San Antonio was no different.

I started eating whatever cookie or snack I came across as I unpacked our kitchen dish-packs. I stopped drinking eight glasses of water a day. We went out for dinner the first week we lived in our new house and I lost my resolve to eat carefully, to keep myself in check, to maintain portion control.

Within a month, I had found some of my lost weight. It was a nightmare.

But I must say that to his credit, John is always very supportive whenever I go on these diets. He wishes that I didn't have to put myself through such drastic measures, over and over again. I can hear the sincerity in his voice when he asks me how my diet is going.

You know what? He really is 'Earnest'!

ଓଃଃ

San Antonio – 1981

We moved into our new San Antonio home in June, and John started the two-year clinical portion of his prosthodontic residency at Wilford Hall Medical Center, Lackland Air Force Base. We bought more ceiling fans, John was able to install them in various rooms and our ceilings remained intact. Whew!

We met another Air Force prosthodontist, Jim Sheets and his wife Beth, and we became great friends. They didn't live too far from us and they enjoyed having 'theme' parties. One day we got an invitation to their Mismatch Party. Everyone was to wear clothing that did not match ... the more outlandish, the better.

One October, the Sheets had a Halloween party. Because I had a long red dress, I went as Mrs. Santa Claus. Tillie, now a Texan in her new cowboy boots, made her San Antonio debut, trusting that military adage "Don't ask, don't tell!"

Despite these shocking photos, John was promoted to lieutenant colonel the following year. Then he got orders to England, which presumably was the Air Force's way of rationalizing, "Pah-leeze! Out of sight, out of mind!"

Merry Olde England-1983

John got orders to RAF Upper Heyford, England. He was going to be the staff prosthodontist in the dental clinic wing of the Air Force hospital. Upper Heyford is about twenty miles north of Oxford, close to the Cotswolds, a charming region known for its quaint towns and thatched cottages, and an hour and a half drive from London.

We were allowed to ship one POV (privately owned vehicle) to England so we sent our Mercedes 240 D sedan. Keep in mind that you drive on the left side of the road in the United Kingdom. Our 240 D's steering wheel was on the left. If I wanted to pass the car in front of me, I had to pull almost all the way out into the right, *oncoming lane* to see if it was safe to pass. Since our Mercedes had little-to-no pick-up, the only thing it passed was … gas. Diesel that is!

We needed a second car so we bought a new, green Toyota Space Cruiser, a futuristic-looking, angular van. The Space Cruiser had British specs so the steering wheel was on the right and therefore, a much safer vehicle for passing. The only problem was that the controls on the steering column were reversed so when John drove it and thought he was putting on the directional signal, he turned on the windshield wipers instead.

At first, I thought I would never learn to drive on the left side of the road. Everyone told me, "Just follow the car in front of you and you'll do fine." So I did and I ended up in Scotland. (Just kidding.) It took a couple of weeks of very cautious, nervous driving but eventually, I got the hang of it.

Except for "essential personnel" who were required to live on the base at RAF Upper Heyford, the majority of the base housing for officers was seven miles away in the town of Bicester (pronounced BIS-ter) at RAF Bicester, a pre-World War II base and glider field.

Bicester base housing was full when we arrived in July of 1983. We put our name on the waiting list and were told that the wait would be at least six months.

Contacting an 'estate agent' (a realtor), we started looking for a place to rent. Our estate agent would meet us at a specific car park (parking lot) in various towns near Upper Heyford and from there we would follow him to see rental homes.

Our first meeting was at a car park in Banbury, the town of "Ride a cock horse, to Banbury cross" fame. Our estate agent was going to show us an "Elizabethan cottage". Oh how wonderful, I thought. It sounded positively charming!

We followed him in our Space Cruiser. We were approaching the northern outskirts of Banbury, when we stopped at a lone house up on a small hill ... across the road from a cemetery.

Besides looking forlorn, the house was small. How small was it? The house was sooooooo small ... I had to *duck* walking through the front door and I am 5'1". John had to limbo!!

We learned that the cottage's thick white plaster walls were subject to "creep", black mold that crept up the walls. The estate agent recommended buying dehumidifiers. The wide-plank wood floors all sloped down towards the cemetery and the walled-in stairwell going up to the second floor bedrooms and bathroom was so narrow that we had to turn sideways.

Yes, this was an 'Elizabethan cottage" all right, as in Elizabeth the FIRST! The cottage had been built sometime between 1575-1600! We had brought our baby grand piano in our household shipment and there was no way our piano would have squeezed into that cottage, much less our queen-size mattress and box spring.

The next day the estate agent showed us a rental home in Oxford but that was more of a commute than John wanted. We looked at other homes closer to Upper Heyford but none were right for us.

Finally, two weeks later, we went to Middle Barton, a small hamlet about eight miles from the base and saw a 3-story townhouse for rent. Being desperate, we rented it.

This photograph of our townhouse was taken by our oldest daughter in 1983. Thanks, Jennifer! Our unit goes from the center of the picture, behind the tree, and to the left.

The downspout behind the tree and the open garage on the left comprise the entire width of the townhouse. Our front door is on the side of the single car garage, which protrudes out from the house. The window to the left of the tree, the two windows above and the skylight in the roof were part of our townhouse, too. However, while narrow, the townhouse was deep. It was like living in three shoeboxes, one box stacked on top of the other.

Because we had to use our single-car garage for storage, we parked our Mercedes in the driveway. We parked the Space Cruiser parallel to the townhouse, half on the sidewalk because the street was so narrow. The Space Cruiser's 15-foot length was almost the width of our townhouse.

We lived there for seven months.

Our front door didn't have a doorknob. We were told that waaaay back in history, doorknobs were taxed! We just inserted a key into a lock, turned it and opened the front door.

Once inside the front door, we stepped into a 4'x4' foyer where we would hang our coats on hooks. Passing from the foyer through the next door, we entered the lounge-diner, a combined living/dining room that extended the entire length of the house. To my delight, the lounge-diner had swirled orange and maroon wall-to-wall carpeting which almost gave me motion sickness.

On the front windows hung lined, maroon velvet drapes, floor to ceiling. Three extra feet of material lay there on the carpet, all bunched up in folds. Call them "Shar- Pei" drapes! The extra material sealed off the drafty front windows and kept the heat in.

We stuffed what furniture we could wall-to-wall in the lounge-diner, each piece abutting the next including our baby grand piano. I stored our coffee table *under* the piano!

A doorway from the lounge-diner led to a small kitchen, which had a sink with individual hot and cold faucets. This allowed me to either scald my hands or freeze them. The oven was in Celsius but fortunately, I had a chart that told me the equivalent conversion temperatures from Celsius to Fahrenheit.

The refrigerator was waist-high and the freezer compartment held two small ice trays and a half-gallon of ice cream. The hot water heater also heated our home and was on a timer. I was barely warm in the house for five hours a day—6-8 a.m. and 6-9 p.m.—otherwise I saw my breath.

A heavy fire door with chicken wire embedded in its glass window opened from the lounge-diner into a stairwell. Climbing seven stairs up to a small landing, turning left and left again, I climbed *another* seven stairs to the second floor where there were three bedrooms, a bathroom with a sink and bathtub and a separate 'loo' room.

Climbing another seven stairs, two more left turns and climbing seven *more* stairs brought me to the third floor and our master bedroom, twenty-eight stairs total ... pant! pant! I can't begin to tell you the number of times I was found sound asleep on the second floor landing!

The master bathroom had a *loo*, a miniscule sink and a tiled shower that was so narrow my shoulders touched the shower walls—like showering in a phone booth.

The skylight in the master bedroom ceiling provided lots of light. It could be tilted open but spiders often spun their webs in the corners of the skylight at night. As you will learn, I absolutely, positively, unequivocally and categorically cannot abide spiders.

The garage was our Public Storage unit, holding additional furniture, bicycles, luggage, cartons stacked from floor-to-ceiling and our queen-size box spring.

Our box spring? Yes, that's right. While we were able to jam, cram, ram and shove our folded queen mattress up the twenty-eight stairs to the third floor, the box spring's wooden frame was too inflexible to go around the stair landings.

As a result, we wound up sleeping on our mattress on the floor for seven months. I thought I was living in Japan.

Most of the appliances we had brought with us operated on 110 volts, 60 cycles/sec or Hertz. (John told me!). British homes were wired with 220 volt, so in order to operate our U.S. appliances without burning them up, we had to buy transformers to convert the higher voltage to a usable power.

Transformers come in different sizes, depending on the size of your appliance, and different weights, but boy, oh boy, they were heavy buggers.

When I cleaned the townhouse, I would go into our small laundry area, pick up our vacuum cleaner with one hand and cradling a 20-pound transformer against me with the other, I climbed those twenty-eight stairs up to our third floor bedroom and started vacuuming, working my way down the stairs, vacuuming them, and every room as I went along.

Being younger back in 1983 and a much more conscientious housekeeper, I vacuumed so often that after living there for seven months, I looked like a very short Arnold Schwarzenegger.

⊗₴⊙

Ham Anyone?

We began adjusting to life in England. We learned that we filled up our cars with 'petrol', that cars had 'bonnets' (hoods), a 'boot' (the trunk) and that when we passed a truck, we had, in fact, passed a 'lorry'.

A month after moving to Middle Barton, John and I went to Blenheim Palace in Woodstock, not far from Oxford, to an outdoor Barry Manilow concert.

Blenheim Palace, the ancestral home of the Duke of Marlborough, was also the birthplace of Winston Churchill. Our youngest daughter Betsy and Winston share the same birth date, the 30th of November. Consequently, Betsy has always felt a certain kinship with Winston, though we were happy when Betsy gave up smoking cigars by the time she was three.

The sight of gypsies was a new experience for us. We would occasionally see their colorful wagons parked along a roadside. There would be a shaggy horse tethered under a tree, a goat tied to a stake, a dog running around, several rather scruffy-looking children playing nearby and a campfire burning close to the wagon. The British called them *Romanies*.

One day after John had left for the dental clinic and the girls were in school, there was a knock at my front door. It was a gypsy. He wanted to know if I had any knives that needed sharpening. I had been told that gypsies often went door-to-door sharpening knives as a way to make money.

I had a good Wusthof carving knife that had become somewhat dull over the years so I brought it to this fellow. He propped his bike up on a U-shaped stand and adjusted it. There was a whetting stone near the back tire. Turning a bike pedal by hand also turned the whetting stone. He held my knife to the stone, sharpened it and charged me 50p (pence)—at the time about 75¢.

From the time I had opened my door until he rode away, only a couple of minutes had passed. But after he left, I realized what a potentially dangerous position I had been in—home alone with a gypsy sharpening my now razor-sharp 12" carving knife. Yikes, what was I thinking???

I had been vaguely familiar with a choral group called the Skylarks, the name of the Air Force officers' wives choir ... gals who enjoyed singing. There were Skylark choirs on many Air Force bases but I had never joined. That changed once we got to England, however.

I joined the Skylarks shortly after we arrived because I had heard that they needed an accompanist. A year later, when the Skylarks' conductor and her husband moved back to the States, I volunteered to be their conductor while accompanying them on the piano.

We performed twice a year for the OWC, the Officer's Wives Club—in December for the Christmas Tea and for the annual "Bring Your British Neighbor" luncheon in the spring. Many American families lived in English villages and the "Bring your British Neighbor" social at the Officers Club, a lovely luncheon with a concert by the Skylarks, was always a special day.

Because I enjoyed Skylarks so much, John decided that he wanted to form a singing group as well. He knew a number of dentists who loved to sing, so he got a group of them together to rehearse. When the Christmas season rolled around that next December, I had both the Skylarks and John's group perform at the Christmas Tea.

John wondered what he could call his group of singing dentists and I came up with their name ... The Drills Brothers!

In addition to working with his dental colleagues, John was responsible for his prosthodontic laboratory staff—the dental technicians who made the crowns, bridges, partial and removable dentures John designed.

The Non-Commissioned Officer in Charge of the lab, (the NCOIC), was Master Sergeant Bill Hutchins who had arrived at Upper Heyford that same summer of 1983. His wife, a teacher, had remained in the States with all but one of their children, although they too eventually moved to Upper Heyford in 1984. Their oldest son, William, had come to England with his father, however, so that he could get started in high school right away.

On December 24, 1983, John, Jennifer, Betsy and I went into London to attend a Christmas Eve service at St. Paul's Cathedral. I had never heard an all-male church choir (men and boys) sing before. Their sound, along with the magnificent pipe organ and the marvelous acoustics of that cathedral, gave my goosebumps goosebumps!

Because MSgt. Hutchins and William were going to be all by

themselves on Christmas Day, John and I had invited them to come to our Middle Barton home for Christmas dinner.

I had bought a whole Gwaltney baked ham in our commissary the week before to be sure that I had plenty for Christmas dinner. The ham came completely wrapped in thick paper and along with other items I purchased, I was ready for Christmas Day.

Jennifer and Betsy set our table festively with Christmas colors and Sgt. Hutchins and William arrived promptly at 6 p.m. We all sat in our 'lounge-diner' to visit while I served appetizers. The baked ham was already cooked when I bought it so basically I was just heating it up.

As everyone else continued visiting in our 'lounge', I asked John to join me in the kitchen. I took the ham out of the oven and setting it on a carving board, I asked John to start slicing.

He cut several thick slices of ham and using the carving knife and fork, he lifted them up and set them down on my large serving platter. But they weren't pink the way baked ham is *supposed* to be. Oh no, they were thick, steaming slices of *GRAY!!!*

I gasped and cupped my hand over my mouth. I told John to cut the ham at the other end, hoping he would find a section where the ham was pink but the ham was gray there too. I didn't know how long that ham had been in the commissary but my heart sank and I felt sick to my stomach.

I had John continue to cut in different areas and he finally found one small section where the ham was pink. Cutting out those chunks, he placed them on my platter—three pitiful, small pink chunks of ham on a platter the size of a hubcap.

"Jennifer. Betsy." I called out. "Would you come into the kitchen, please?"

"Look, girls," I whispered, "I don't know what's wrong with the ham. It's gray. We only have a few pieces that are pink and look okay. I don't want you to take any ham because I won't have enough. Just help yourself to the green beans, rolls, yams and pineapple, okay?"

John tried a piece of the gray ham and said it tasted okay but I wasn't about to put gray ham on my platter. Finding a few more areas of pink, John chunked it out while I got out a much much smaller serving plate and then called everyone to the table for dinner.

While John said "Grace", I asked the Almighty to "please, please, please, please" let my ham, our friends and John be okay.

Thankfully, we all enjoyed the meal and all was well.

You know, Dear Reader, this reminds me. I am so grateful that friends like you have purchased my book that I want to invite you all over for dinner one of these days as well.

But I just need to know …

What *color* do you like your ham?

RAF Bicester – 1984

We finally got word from the Housing Office that a home at RAF Bicester would become available in February. We were delighted and in February 1984, we moved from Middle Barton to RAF Bicester.

Our home at 14 Blencowe Close was a two-story, all brick house with a yellow front door. With four bedrooms and one and a half bathrooms, it had a separate *loo* room with the water tank mounted up high on the wall. In order to flush the *loo*, you had to pull a long chain coming from the tank so that gravity provided the necessary water pressure to clean 'er out.

The house was also compartmentalized—there was a doorway from the hallway into the kitchen, another doorway into the living room, another into the dining room. However, this was a much larger, more spacious home ... no third floor or skylight to contend with. The following picture shows our RAF Bicester home with our Toyota Space Cruiser van parked in the driveway:

In 1985, I learned about Jago Stone, a British chap who was making the rounds in our military housing neighborhood. I was told that he would sketch our home for a very reasonable price.

Jago Stone, born in 1928, was more than an artist. In his younger days he had been a scoundrel, a reprobate ... a THIEF! Known as The Silver King, Jago would dress in a monk's cassock, cozy up to some unsuspecting clergyman and whatever his spiel, would have the vicar show him the church's silver. Jago would then return to the church later and steal it!

One time, and almost caught 'in the act', Jago had hidden under the altar for nine hours before he could do his dastardly work—swiping silver chalices, silver communion plates, silver altar candlesticks and whatever else of value he could snatch.

On another occasion in passing himself off as a monk, Jago was so convincing that the vicar asked him to give the sermon the following Sunday!

Jago spent 15 years in prison for his life of crime and it was there that he discovered his remarkable talent for painting. He had found a new calling.

In addition to painting during his post-prison life, Jago also wrote two books: *The Diary of a Cad*, about himself, and *The Burglar's Bedside Companion*—a 'How To' guide for any aspiring crook. What a character!

Jago came to paint our RAF Bicester home one day in the summer of 1985. Before he put brush to canvas however, he asked for a sandwich and a cup of tea—his standard request whenever he painted someone's home. He then sipped and nibbled away as he sat out in a lawn chair on our front yard and sketched our house. He even included our Space Cruiser, which was parked in our driveway that day.

We hang Jago's painting of our British home wherever we live. He charged £50 or a little over $50. Not bad for a cad, *eh wot?*

Number Fourteen: Blencowe Close: R.A.F. Bicester
The Rogerson Family English Home
Jago Stone - 1985

Windsor Great Park

Once we settled into our Bicester home and winter had turned to spring, we began taking daytrips throughout the United Kingdom. We visited beautiful Bath and Salisbury Cathedral. At Stonehenge, we stood in awe at that ancient site. We drove to Wales and found some of my Probyn relatives.

John and I attended Trooping the Colour, the impressive ceremony in London that marks the official birthday of the Queen, and held on the enormous Horse Guards parade ground. We watched regimental troops ride on horseback, and massed bands and other troops march around the parade ground.

The ceremony, while extremely colorful, was quite long and got boring. The monotony of the parade was broken as we watched some of the less fortunate troops step in huge piles of 'road apples'— souvenirs of the horses in the parade. Those on foot must have been highly disciplined because absolutely no consideration was given to breaking rank to avoid those steaming hazards!

On a trip to northern England, we got to meet the famous Scottish veterinarian and author James Herriot, whose wonderful, heart-warming books include *All Creatures Great and Small*, *All Things Bright and Beautiful* among others. If you are an animal lover and have never read any of his books, I recommend them highly. You will love them.

We went to Wimbledon several times and saw incredible matches played by Martina Navratilova and Pam Shriver along with many other world-class tennis players.

During the summers of 1984, 1985 and 1986, we 'drove' to Europe. Well, not exactly 'drove'. We drove to Dover, boarded a ferry across the English Channel to Calais, France. And once there, and in our Space Cruiser van, we drove all around Europe.

Our parents came to visit when we lived in England, giving us wonderful opportunities to play tour guide.

When my parents visited in the summer of 1984, we took them to Wales and introduced them to my father's long-lost relatives, whom we had met previously. The Welsh Probyns were very gracious and welcoming and we were able to maintain written correspondence with them for years.

Since both of my parents loved to play golf, we also took them to St. Andrews, Scotland, where the four of us played The Old Course. It was a thrill for all of us despite the fact that I spent an inordinate amount of time trying to get out of bunkers that were 15' deep!

We went to Scotland one New Year's to celebrate Hogmanay, the Scottish word for the last day of the year. While the girls and I bought small, inexpensive souvenirs for our print boxes, John spent £40 (about $60 at the time) buying ... what else ... old Scottish bagpipes!

I videotaped John playing his 'pipes' one summer in our back garden (backyard) in Bicester. Dressed in his finest tartan kilt (a wrap-around red bath towel), a white t-shirt, knee-high wool socks complete with two Sgian Dubh (butter knives), a sporran (a small purse) around his waist and a plaid beret, John treated the neighborhood to the most humorous Highland Fling and the most gosh-awful bagpipe drone imaginable. Birds flew out of the trees by the hundreds and cats and dogs ran for cover. Minutes later, an ambulance pulled up in front of our house. Two doctors came racing out, asking how many ears had been wounded. ☺ The video is priceless!

In the summer of 1984, another American family, the Wiles, moved into our Bicester housing area just one house away from ours—Cathy, Roger and their three children, Laura, Andrew and Paul. We soon became great friends.

Cathy and I walked around the RAF glider field nearby, after our children went to school. It was a good 4-mile trek, and we walked in rain, shine or freezing fog. We often walked twice a day in the summertime when it stayed light until 10 p.m. I think our jaws got the most exercise because Cathy and I talked and shared stories about ourselves and our lives. I once calculated that we walked about 1,000 miles every year for three years. That's a heap a' talkin'!

Living in England, we learned about quaint English teashops that served scones with jam and clotted cream. Cathy, an excellent cook who loved to host beautiful dinner parties, once mentioned that it might be fun to own a teashop. Since I make a delicious angel food cake (see *Don't Set the Alarm*). I thought that was a great idea and said perhaps we could open a teashop together in Canterbury.

"Canterbury? Why Canterbury?" she asked.

"Well," I replied, "because we could call it" ... are you ready for this? ... " 'The Cup and Chaucer'."

I don't know about you, but I have been given a couple of nicknames over the years. Our daughter Betsy had started calling me "Sheh" to make me smile and to put me in a better frame of mind when she wanted my permission to do something. Bunny, my college roommate, called me "Sher" during our four years at Douglass College. Now it was Cathy's turn.

Over the years and after meeting me, for some reason people have trouble remembering my name and call me "Shirley". It became a joke between Cathy and me. Since I am from New Jersey, Cathy started calling me "Shoiley" or "Shoil" in her best "New Joisey" accent.

Every day for a week in June, the Queen and members of the Royal Family were driven in Bentleys from Windsor Castle down the "Long Walk", a 2.5-mile drive in Windsor Great Park. At a certain location, they transferred into horse-drawn carriages and proceeding through the park, waved to the viewing public as they headed to Royal Ascot for the horse races.

The Wiles had attended this Royal Procession twice before and along with Roger's squadron, we got to go a couple of times as well.

Taking picnic baskets and blankets, we all spread out on the grass alongside the road and ate our lunch as we awaited the Royal Family Procession. British citizens and schoolchildren, dressed in their traditional school uniforms, lined the road with us while Bobbies patrolled both on foot and horseback.

Not long after finishing our lunch, we heard the clip-clop of approaching horses. John videotaped the procession while Jennifer and Betsy took the following pictures.

The last photo is especially meaningful.

104 | Page   Living with the Late John Rogerson

Living with the Late John Rogerson　　　　　Page | 105

And the following year:

Seeing The Royal Procession was so exciting! The whole 'parade' moved along at a good clip and didn't last more than a couple of minutes, but what a memorable experience.

What a thrill it was to see Queen Elizabeth, Prince Phillip and Prince Andrew ... this close!

The Queen Mum was always a crowd favorite. She beamed and waved as she passed by.

Fergie, in her round brimmed hat and waving a gloved hand, was much in favor back then. She certainly isn't anymore.

We had so much fun that we returned the following year. As you see, Queen Elizabeth was wearing a different outfit and a different hat that year. I suppose it was because she didn't want us to see her in the same outfit twice.

The last photo shows Princess Diana in happier days, before her life ended so tragically.

She and Prince Charles had been married for three years at this point and their first son, Prince William, was only two years old.

I would imagine that The Royal Family does not ride through Windsor Great Park in open-air carriages anymore. In our post- 9/11 world, this Royal Procession would be an absolute security nightmare.

But weren't we fortunate to have been stationed at Upper Heyford during these years.

Seeing the Royal Family and their Royal Procession was definitely a highlight during our four-year tour.

❧❦

Arachnophobia

Who's afraid of spiders … can I have a show of hands?

Yup, me too. I am terrified of those 8-legged creatures. As far as I'm concerned, if I am sharing a room with a spider, one of us soon will be dead and I don't mean just dead. I mean deader-than-dead: sprayed with RAID until completely white, then clobbered and crushed. Whew … I get the willies just thinking about them.

I really don't know what it is about spiders that scares the living daylights out of me, but I am unable to resume any activity if I see one. It must DIE. If the spider is on the carpet, not too large and readily accessible, I'll step on it. By not too large I mean shirt-button size … STOMP!STOMP!STOMP! I might even grind it into the carpet for good measure, provided, of course, that I am wearing shoes. R.I.P Spider … Rest In Pieces!

If a spider is lurking in a corner or is on the ceiling, not easily 'do-awayable', well that's a different story. That's where my can of dandy concentrated insect spray (RAID for Wasp and Hornet) comes in handy. I keep a can of RAID in every room in our house. Goodness knows, I could see a spider along a baseboard only to find it has disappeared while I run to another room to get the RAID.

When a spider, thoroughly covered in RAID, drops from the ceiling from sheer added weight, it meets with continued bad luck as my foot descends upon it … KA-POW! When we had a fireplace, the 'KA-POW' was achieved with the shovel from our fireplace set … WHACKA!WHACKA!WHACKA!!! The spider, suffering a severe headache at this point, was then gingerly wiped up and flushed away. *Au revoir, Charlotte!*

I am always on the lookout for spiders. John says my head is like one of those radar screens you see on the top of an airport control tower, sweeping from side-to-side as I scan a room for any dark spot that could be a spider. I am so paranoid about spiders that if I see a picture of one in a magazine or newspaper, I have to fold that page over so that I can't see it and to keep it from crawling off the printed page and into my lap … EEEEEEEEYIKES!!!!

One day, I walked our dog Barney on his leash on a narrow strip of newly laid sod along the side yard of our new San Antonio home. Keeping an eye on Barney, who was quite elderly and unsteady on his feet, we were slowly making our way around the grass when I suddenly FROZE.

There, right in front of us and not more than three feet away, was an unwanted visitor from the overgrown, vacant lot next door ... a living, breathing, hairy and terrifying ... TARANTULA! Just writing this description makes my hands clammy!

My heart began pounding and I started hyperventilating. I could barely move and even if I could, I knew that Barney would not be able to keep up with me. I just knew that the tarantula was going to come after us.

Looking around, I found a short, thick tree limb on the ground. I picked it up and took small steps towards my adversary. In slow motion, I raised my makeshift weapon and WHAMA! WHAMA!WHAMA!, I pulverized that tarantula to Kingdom Come. I tell you, I beat it like a woman possessed!

I was drenched. My knees had turned to jelly and I felt like I had just run a marathon. It had been, "One small step for mankind, one less step for Mr. Tarantula."

Turning to Barney, I felt badly that he had had to witness this horrific scene but it was a needless concern. Totally unaware of the unfolding drama, Barney's nose had been sniffing out a new potty location!

Every summer during our tour in England, we took a family vacation on the European mainland. We would cross the English Channel by ferry and in our van, would spend three weeks or so sightseeing.

One summer, we drove through France and Belgium to Germany. We toured Neuschwanstein, the castle nestled in the Bavarian Alps and the model for Disney's Cinderella Castle. We toured Hitler's Eagle's Nest in Bertsgarten and visited the beautiful Royal Palace of Herrenchiemsee. The majestic snowcapped mountains, brilliant blue lakes, colorful chalets and window boxes overflowing with flowers were all spectacular!

Our vacation almost over, we were back in France touring the famous Palace of Versailles. Our English-speaking guide had us gather around her in an enormous foyer just inside the palace entrance.

John, Jennifer, Betsy and I—part of a group of about thirty people—were taking the "Everything You *Never* Wanted To Know About Versailles Tour". With her French accent, our guide was a little difficult to understand as she peppered us with more facts, figures, names, dates and other minutiae than one finds in a baseball almanac! You are probably getting the picture that I am not exactly a museum person.

The truth is, on a tour or in a museum, I just want to learn the three most pertinent facts, see the three most photographed rooms, view the three most important works of art and then I'm 'outta there'!

Our guide droned on ... and on ... and on. Jennifer rolled her eyes at me. I made a 'Limburger-cheese face' by wrinkling up my nose at Betsy. We all watched John who was listening intently, trying to absorb all the information this guide was imparting—the same John who can't remember what he did yesterday!

"Mesdames et Messieurs," our guide announced, "if you vill gazzer over by zee bust of Louis XVI at zee far end of zee hall, ve can begin zee tour." Like sheep, we shuffled our way over to the larger-than-life bust of Louis XVI, whose curly locks would have made Shirley Temple jealous.

The four of us stood at the back of our group as the guide yammered on when suddenly, something caught my eye.

A woman with tightly permed brown hair was standing in front of me and like John, she was engrossed in the guide's presentation. But eeeGADS! There was a small black spider crawling all over her head, going from curl to curl!

My eyes got as big as saucers. How could this woman not know something was moving around her head? I nudged Jennifer who nudged Betsy and the three of us stood there, staring with our mouths wide open, as the woman seemed oblivious.

I touched John's arm to get his attention, nodded towards the woman and mouthed, "spider ... on ... her ... head."

John looked over and saw the spider working its way over her curls. Reaching up, he grabbed and squeezed the spider between his thumb and index finger and flung the dead insect to the floor, missing nary word of the guide's discourse.

It was good to see the spider 'done in' but now what were we three girls going to do for the rest of the tour? The show was over. Charlotte was dead!

We moved to Sheppard Air Force Base in Wichita Falls, Texas in 1990 and lived in base housing.

In my PJs and ready for bed one night, I had just propped my pillow up behind me to read when a spider ... an ENORMOUS spider ... leapt ... no VAULTED ... out from behind my bookcase and ran under my nightstand.

I screamed and to my surprise, suddenly found myself standing upright in the middle of our bed. How I got there, I don't know, but levitation must have played a part!

My scream had come from somewhere deep within me, down from the core of my being and it brought John running into our bedroom, asking, **"What was that? What's the matter?"**

"Under my nightstand!" I gasped. "Spider ... HUGE!"

"Oh, for goodness sakes." John sighed, got down on his hands and knees, and peered under my nightstand. "I don't see a thing."

"Look along the baseboard and under the bed" I pleaded. I had grabbed my pillow and clutching it, I pulled our headboard away from the wall and looked down along the baseboard, walking back and forth across our mattress like a caged animal.

"The spider isn't going to hurt you." John said soothingly. "It is more afraid of you than you are of it." (I have always loved that one.) "Just forget about it," he suggested.

FORGET ABOUT IT? Was he nuts!! "Please pull the sweater boxes out from under the bed. Maybe it's hiding between them."

"Why don't you go sleep in Jennifer's bed if you can't sleep here," John suggested.

"I am NOT leaving this bedroom until I know that spider is dead, otherwise it'll just be here in the morning. I'll turn this room upside down and inside out if I have to." (I wasn't really prepared to do that ... I wanted JOHN to do it!)

John let out a groan, but being a good husband, he got down on his hands and knees again and looked under his side of the bed, all the while muttering about how silly I was and how foolish this hunt was.

All of a sudden he said, "Hand me a flashlight please and the insect spray." I jumped off the end of our bed, got a flashlight and handed him the RAID.

"What? Do you see it? It's big, isn't it. Is it there? Can you—"

PSSSSSST went the can of RAID. "Did you get it? Is it moving? Get it, get it, get it!"

The spider took off running under the bed back to my side. I jumped back on the bed. "GET IT!GET IT!GET IT!!!!" I pleaded.

John ran around the bed to my side and as the spider emerged, he stepped on it ... once. He picked it up with a tissue and flushed it away.

Climbing on his white horse, John galloped off into the sunset, leaving me wondering, "Who *was* that masked man? Oh yes, My Hero!"

Green Around the Gills

As previously mentioned, every summer John, Jennifer, Betsy and I would drive to the port at Dover, board a ferry to cross the English Channel to Calais and travel around Europe in our van for two or three weeks. How neat was that!

In the summer of 1984, we took our very first trip to the Continent and thought it might be fun taking the hovercraft instead of a ferry. While more expensive than going by ferry, it was considerably faster—35 minutes versus 90.

A hovercraft is what I'll call an 'airborne ferry'. Turbine engines generate massive amounts of air, which fill rubber skirts encircling the hull. These skirts in turn lift the hovercraft above the water, allowing huge propellers on top of the ship to skim the water and 'fly' it across the Channel at speeds of up to 58mph.

Hovercrafts are completely enclosed. With airline-style seating lining each side of the ship holding several hundred passengers, the interior of the ship can hold up to 60 cars. The crossing was called a 'flight', the ship's captain was called the 'pilot' and 'flight attendants' attended to passenger needs.

On a lovely summer morning in 1984, we drove to Dover. The English Channel was calm, barely rippling, and it sparkled like diamonds in the bright sunshine. Our hovercraft crossing, while rather noisy, was quick and easy. It was definitely a unique experience and despite the increased cost, we vowed to do it again someday.

That day came two years later. But before reading further, let me warn you ... you may want to take some Dramamine.

It was the summer of 1986 and we were planning our annual 'road trip' to Europe. Remembering how much we had enjoyed our hovercraft crossing in 1984, we decided to do it again but in reverse. Once our vacation was over, we would take the hovercraft from Calais back to Dover.

We had a great time touring Europe but inevitably, our vacation ended and it was time to go home. We had reservations to take the 5 p.m. hovercraft 'flight' back to England.

On our way to Calais, I noticed dark, ominous-looking clouds hugging the entire English coastline, twenty-six miles in the distance. My stomach tightened and I began to gnaw my lower lip.

We arrived at the Port of Calais around 3:30 p.m., but by then, the cloud ceiling had lowered to the point where I could no longer see England at all, the sun had disappeared and the Channel was churning with whitecaps. I started working on my upper lip.

The hovercraft ticket agent who confirmed our 5 p.m. reservation said that weather conditions were deteriorating rapidly but that if we hurried, we could get on the 4 p.m. crossing to avoid a possible cancellation of our scheduled 'flight'. We took it.

The 4 p.m. hovercraft was already parked on a huge concrete parking lot near the water's edge and we were instructed to drive our van into the middle section of the ship. Leaving it, we walked to the port side of the ship and took our seats. Jennifer and Betsy sat together next to one of the large plate glass windows while John and I sat across the aisle from them, in a row that held four people.

Once everyone was on board, the engines revved up and the hull skirts inflated, billowing out around the ship. The pilot turned the hovercraft around and "taxied" into the water. Flight attendants went around checking to see that our seatbelts were fastened tightly.

Initially, everything went smoothly as we moved out into the water protected by a long jetty, but beyond it, the Channel waters were being whipped ... oh, wait. Have you taken some Dramamine yet?

You may wonder if I am subject to motion sickness. Let me count the ways!

When I was a child and had to sit in the backseat of our family car, I got carsick all the time. I can feel queasy in an elevator when it arrives at the requested floor and it starts slowing, but then dropping ever so slightly, before inching back up to the exact stopping point ... Urp! I even have trouble eating on a moored ship. One time we were going to have lunch on a tethered ferryboat in Corpus Christi, Texas. While imperceptible to most, the slight rocking motion of the waves made my stomach flip-flop to the point that food was the last thing I wanted to think about. I had to get off the ferryboat and back on *terra firma* pronto.

As I was saying, before I so rudely interrupted myself, now we were about to cross the English Channel whose waters were being whipped into a frenzy by strong winds. Once beyond the protection of the jetty, the hovercraft started bucking immediately. I grabbed my armrests and spread my feet apart to keep my balance.

Two minutes into our 'flight', the pilot announced that instead of taking us directly across the Channel to England, he was going to head south and parallel the French coast in hopes of finding less 'choppy' waters to make the crossing. Choppy? Choppy my foot!

The Channel got rougher and the hovercraft began to roll from side-to-side and pitch from stem to stern. Enormous waves splashed against the windows and passengers began crying out with each motion ... *"Oooooooh.Ooooooh.Ooooooh"*.

Flight attendants staggered up and down the aisle, grabbing the backs of seats for support, as they took orders for cold water while reassuring us that the hovercraft was perfectly safe, that we were not in any danger. I heard the man sitting behind me, whimpering.

After what seemed like an eternity, the pilot announced that he was going to head west, toward England. And that's when we hit the storm's fury head-on.

With the English Channel in full boil, massive waves and sprays of foam dashed against the windows as the hovercraft plunged down into the water, then rose up again on the next massive wave crest.

Hallucinating, I thought I saw Charon the ferryman, taking souls of the dead across the river Styx to the gates of the underworld—to Hades.

John grabbed an' upchuck' bag for me but I managed, through clenched teeth, to utter "no". He saw that Betsy was holding a bag up to Jennifer. Many passengers were getting sick. The retching sounds and the resultant smell filled the hovercraft. Some passengers were crying out, "HELP! HELP! HELP!" while others just cried.

Not me though. I couldn't do that. I sat frozen—in a state of rigor mortis. I stared straight ahead and I am not sure that I was even breathing. I pressed my head back against the headrest as hard as I could to keep it locked in position and squeezed my armrests with all my might. Every muscle in my body, including my eyeballs, was as tense and tight as the strings on a tennis racquet. John fanned me vigorously with an in-flight magazine but I was too far gone to notice.

I was so rigid that if I had been dropped from the ceiling, I would have shattered into a million pieces. I never once felt nauseous because my stomach had knotted into a solid ball.

John wasn't worried though, he never got sick. Being an eternal optimist, it would not have surprised me if John had suddenly stood up, stepped out into the aisle and with a big smile, started singing:

♫ "On the goo-oo-ood ship Lollipop, ♫
It's a sweet trip to a candy shop.
Where bon-bons play,
♫ On the sunny beach of Dover and Calais!" ♫

Our crossing did not take 35 or 45 or even 60 minutes. It took 90 minutes to get across the Channel and inside the curved jetty at the Port of Dover. That's when our pilot came on over the intercom, apologizing for the extremely rough crossing.

Once the hovercraft was positioned on the concrete parking ramp, everyone prepared to get off, except me. I couldn't stand up. I was so stiff and my muscles were so tense that John and another passenger had to lock arms and carry me off the hovercraft. They set me down on the parking lot.

John, Jennifer and Betsy piled into our van and drove to where I sat on the tarmac. John had to pick me up, put me in the van and buckle my seatbelt. It was a 4+-hour drive back to Bicester. I spent the entire time massaging my thighs with my hands, rocking back and forth and saying, "I can't get my muscles to relax. I can't get my legs to relax."

Once back in Bicester, I crawled upstairs to our bathroom, filled our bathtub with hot water and climbed in. It didn't help. I could not walk normally or stand up straight for the next three days.

I learned later that after John sat me down on the hovercraft's parking area in Dover, he went into their Administration Building to use the men's room. While there, he inquired about our ordeal and learned that *after* our 4 p.m. departure, all other Channel crossings, both hovercraft and ferry, had been cancelled and would not resume until the storm subsided.

The Beaufort Wind Scale– used by Britain's Royal Navy since 1805 to measure sea conditions, wave heights and wind speeds—goes from 0 to 12 with 12 being the worst. John was told that we had crossed the Channel in a Force 9 gale with sustained winds of 47-54 mph.

When I finally recovered, I promised myself that I would never, *EVER* put myself through that again.

Now we live in Florida where folks go on cruises all the time. Friends have wanted us to join them and have wondered why I won't.

Well, folks ... now you know.

The thought of a cruise brings back such terrifying memories that I just can't bring myself to do it, period.

Even though Charon the ferryman was *not* our pilot that day, our hovercraft crossing back to England was ninety minutes of pure Hades!

◦§◦

Real Estate Moguls

John was promoted to full colonel in 1986 and we were thrilled. His 'pinning-on ceremony', when eagle insignias could officially be put on his shoulders, was quite a day and I had a promotion party for him a week later.

In 1987, shortly before we left England to move back to the United States, we were able to take advantage of Jennifer and Betsy's high school spring break to go on another family trip. We did a 'house swap' with an Air Force dentist and his family stationed in Greece! They flew to London while we flew to Athens and we lived in each other's homes for a week.

Unfortunately, we had unseasonably cool, cloudy weather the entire time we were there, but what a thrill it was to see the Acropolis and walk around the Parthenon. We stood on the top of Lycabettus Hill for a wonderful panoramic view of the city and saw ancient treasures in the National Archaeological Museum. Maintaining my philosophy about museums, I made sure I saw their three most significant exhibits.

We enjoyed Greek food and one day took a cruise to the islands of Aegina, Poros and Hydra. The girls and I bought a couple of souvenirs for our print boxes and fortunately John never saw any Greek bagpipes for sale … "*Chari sto Theo*" (Thanks be to God!).

We flew back to the United States in July 1987. John had orders to McGuire Air Force Base in Wrightstown, New Jersey.

Initially moving into base housing at McGuire, we knew that we would be in New Jersey for three years so we decided to buy a home.

At first, we concentrated our search in Princeton, knowing that living in such an upscale community would keep property values high and increase the potential value of our investment.

Unfortunately, the town was too rich for our blood, so we settled for a 1950s, tri-level house at 8 Windsor Drive in Princeton Junction, on the other side of the tracks!

Even so, we paid $225,000 … almost 2 ½ times what we had paid for our San Antonio home. To add to the financial hardship, John's commute to the base was 30 miles each way.

In the three years we lived at 8 Windsor Drive, we remodeled and painted the *entire* house, inside and out, doing all the work ourselves. We painted and/or wallpapered every surface that didn't move. Recruiting our daughters, when they were home from college one summer and when they weren't waitressing at TGI Fridays, we had them help us paint the exterior.

John renovated the knotty pine kitchen, installing new appliances and overhead lighting. He remodeled the main bathroom completely, doing all the plumbing and electrical work himself. He designed and built a fieldstone walkway up to our front door and completely re-landscaped the front of our house.

In the summer of 1990, John got orders to Sheppard Air Force Base in Wichita Falls, Texas, to report in October.

Our daughters, who had been going to Rutgers University in New Brunswick, transferred to Texas A&M University in College Station, Texas. They were going to live together so we drove them down to College Station that August to help set up their apartment.

Yet again, we were unable to sell our house. The real estate market had taken a hit and was in a major slump. We ended up renting our home to various families for the next five years, until we finally got a call from our realtor saying that she had found a buyer.

Here's the painful conclusion: we paid $225,000 for the home in 1987, spent every moment of three years and approximately $60,000 renovating it and walked away at closing some $86,000 poorer!

Anyone care to borrow our real estate "Karma"? If we had ever had it, it was "Kompletely Kaput!"

CR$O

Howdy and Aloha! - 1990 - 1991

In October of 1990, John and I drove in separate cars from New Jersey to Sheppard Air Force Base in northern Texas. Howdy, y'all! We were able to move into a base house at 239 Polaris Street right away.

By the time we arrived, Jennifer and Betsy were well into their classes at Texas A&M. Taking a break from emptying cartons and settling in, about a week later, we drove the 300 miles south to College Station to see them.

A month later, Jennifer and Betsy came "home" for Thanksgiving to a brand new city, a new Air Force Base, a new house and to their new bedrooms, none of which they had ever seen before. How strange is that! But that can be the life of military "brats".

I loved living on base again and John enjoyed the short commute to the dental clinic. With so much in common with military folks all around us, we quickly made many new friends.

After feeling reasonably settled, we attended the First United Methodist Church in downtown Wichita Falls for the first time, to see what it was like. Because John filled out the Visitors' card, that *same* Sunday afternoon the associate minister, John Dillard, paid us a visit.

It just so happened that the evening before, John had started working on a project in our living room. Since his job at Sheppard included lecturing dental residents, he had spread out *hundreds* of stone casts of patient's teeth *all over our living room carpet.* He was organizing them for use in demonstrations when lecturing the residents on his specialty, Prosthodontics, and he had left the casts out all night long. It looked like John had dug up a cemetery!

When Reverend Dillard walked into our living room that afternoon, I am sure he thought he had entered the catacombs of Rome!

In mid-1991, John told me that he wanted us to spend two weeks in Hawaii to celebrate our 25th wedding anniversary! While I had always wanted to go to Hawaii, the thought of having to fly made me somewhat less enthusiastic about the venture. In fact, I dreaded it.

John, ever the optimist, didn't let *my* reservations interfere with *his* reservations for us to stay at the Hale Koa on Oahu. The Hale Koa is a military hotel right on Waikiki Beach and he booked it so that we would definitely be there on our anniversary, the 3rd of September.

We flew to Hawaii in late August. As soon as we got to our room and changed clothes, we headed out to the beach. I couldn't wait to see the famous Diamond Head and sure enough, there it was. Aloha!

Once we got to Hawaii, I was thrilled. The next day I waded in front of the Hale Koa while John swam. I wore my one and only bathing suit, which I still have ... AND WILL NOT GET RID OF until it gets holes in the knees!

It is a well-known fact that you can't leave Hawaii until you have visited Hilo Hattie's, the famous shop that sells everything Hawaiian. You name it, Hilo Hattie's has it. Besides other purchases, we bought matching Hawaiian shirts so that folks would look at us and say, "Awww, look at the 'twin-ners'"!

The Hilton Hawaiian Village and Hotel is right next to the Hale Koa and very convenient for seeing any of their shows. We walked over to the hotel one evening and who do you think we saw? Here's a clue:

♪ Tiny bubbles ... in the wine,
Makes me happy. Makes me feel fine....♪

Right, Lawrence Welk! No, I know you got it right. It was Don Ho. John wanted to have our picture taken with him....

…but not nearly as much as John wanted to have *his* picture taken with the performer we saw at the Hilton the following week. Say "Cuchi-Cuchi!"

On the 3rd of September, we celebrated our 25th anniversary with dinner in the Hale Koa, followed by a magic show in their auditorium. At the show, our table of 10 learned about our special celebration (probably because I told them!). They, in turn, told the magician who called John up to the stage to assist him with a trick. Locking John in a vertical box, the magician proceeded to pierce the box with long steel swords from every conceivable direction. Ouch! When the swords were removed, John stepped out of the box, unscathed, but I noticed he left a wet trail behind him every time he took a drink of water.

When we returned to our room after the show, I asked John to get out his camera and his shorty pajamas.

It was *exactly* 25 years since our wedding day and *exactly* 25 years since John had taken my picture wearing his shorty pajamas on our wedding night in Bermuda, as you might remember from *Don't Set the Alarm!* ...

September 3, 1966:

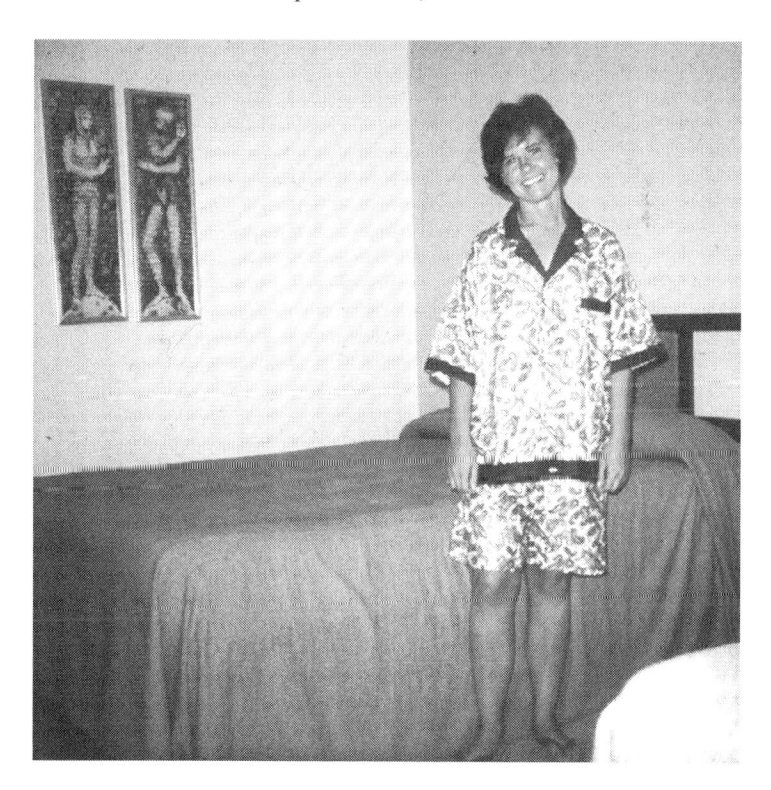

And 25 years later - September 3rd, 1991:

Like the puzzle you find in the newspaper, see if you can pick out 6 differences between the two pictures ... although I can only find 5, myself. The pajamas are different, I'm wearing slippers instead of flip-flops, the bedspreads are different, my hands are on my hips and the pictures of Adam and Eve have been replaced with a flowered picture on a different wall. How did you do? Other than that, I look exactly the same though, don't you think? ☺

During our two weeks in Hawaii, we rented a car and drove all over Oahu. We went to Pearl Harbor and toured the USS Arizona Memorial. We visited the Dole Pineapple Plantation and spent half a day at the Polynesian Cultural Center. We drove to Waimea Bay on Oahu's North Shore, famous for its monstrous waves and surfing competitions. We hiked to the top of Diamond Head where we had fantastic views of Honolulu. We also went to the Neal S. Blaisdall Concert Hall one evening to hear the Honolulu Symphony in concert.

Another day we decided to go to Hanauma Bay, known for its great snorkeling. Home to over 400 species of fish, Hanauma Bay, as you see in the picture below, is actually an old volcano crater next to the Pacific Ocean. Over millions of years, the crater rim eroded and washed away, allowing the Pacific to rush in and fill the large bay with fish, coral reefs and sandbars.

It is a great place to snorkel and that's exactly what we did after renting flippers, masks and snorkels.

Not comfortable in water over my head, I made sure that wouldn't happen so I snorkeled as close to shore as possible in water that was 3-inches deep. I could still stand up!

Here is Mr. Snorkel himself:

Note the camera that John is holding. It is a Kodak waterproof, disposable camera for taking underwater photos of all the colorful fish we were told we would see:

One fish, two fish,
Striped fish, yellow fish.
Three fish, red fish,
Blue fish, many fish!

Thank you, Doctor Sherri Seuss.

At first, we both snorkeled close to the beach.

However, John had heard about a sandbar further out in the bay where there were supposed to be some very impressive, colorful fish. While I returned to our beach blanket to read, John snorkeled out to it, taking underwater photographs as he went along.

John loved floating on the water's surface, head down, bobbing along, seeing the different kinds of fish and coral. He was completely unaware that he was about to have a "Kodak moment."

As he approached the sandbar, John suddenly discovered that his feet could touch the sand so he stood up.

Directly in front of him was a sight that literally took John's breath away.

Gasping for breath, John thought he had died and gone to Heaven. But then his photographic instincts took over and Click! went his camera.

After snapping this picture, John slid back down under the water like a submarine, quietly and silently.

If I told you this was me, would you believe it? No, I wouldn't either.

I don't know about you, but this photograph makes me think of the song "Moon River".

I am surprised that this gal did not hear John's gasp; that it didn't alert her to the fact that John, a total stranger, was almost directly behind her … and I do mean "behind"!

Even though *this* photograph is a little light-struck, this gal is apparently not concerned *in the least* about being over-exposed!!!

♥

Sheppard Memories - 1990-1995

Several significant events occurred during the five years we were stationed at Sheppard Air Force Base. In 1993, our parents each had their 50th wedding anniversaries and we had them join us in Texas so we could celebrate, too. John and I both turned 50 during those years as well and had surprise birthday parties for each other ... a lot of fun!

Our daughter Jennifer met and began dating Chris Azzano, a fine young man, then in pilot training, and now one of *the* outstanding fighter pilots in the Air Force. I would fly with him any day. And believe me, for a fear-of-flying mother-in-law to say that, he must be special! They were married at the First United Methodist Church in 1994.

And over the years, Jennifer and Chris have given us two wonderful grandchildren, Allison and Steven, who, by the time this book goes to press, will be 14 and 12 years old respectively. I figure by the time this book hits the Best Seller list, Allison and Steven will be pushing 97 and 95!

Our big day came in July 1995. With a Pass-In-Review military parade, John retired from the Air Force after being on active duty for over twenty-eight years. It had been an incredible ride, a life-changing experience, but now it was time to move on to the next chapter in our lives so ... we moved to Oregon!

John had been hired by the very large dental practice Permanente Dental Associates to be a prosthodontist in their Tigard Dental Clinic, a suburb of Portland.

After we arrived, we rented an apartment in nearby Lake Oswego so that we could get to know the 'lay of the land' before purchasing a home.

Two months later, in October of 1995, John was given the opportunity to attend the American College of Prosthodontists Conference in Washington, D.C.

Deciding to take advantage of this trip back to the east coast, we flew out a few days early to visit our parents still living in New Jersey. John also registered to run in the Marine Corps Half-Marathon in Washington, D.C., along with our daughter Betsy. After that, we were going to head south to Seymour-Johnson Air Force Base in Goldsboro, North Carolina to visit with Jennifer and Chris, then stationed there.

What follows is an account of that never-to-be-forgotten trip.

Does everyone have their seatbelts fastened? Hold on ....

CR80

✈ My Odyssey - October 1995 ✈

Do you remember what I'll call "The Odyssey of the Olympic Torch Relay" ten years ago? Remember when thousands of people helped carry the lit Olympic Torch around the country (map below) on a zigzagging journey before ending in Salt Lake City, the site of the Olympic Games back in 2002? Talk about a 'torch-uous' trek! (Ouch!).

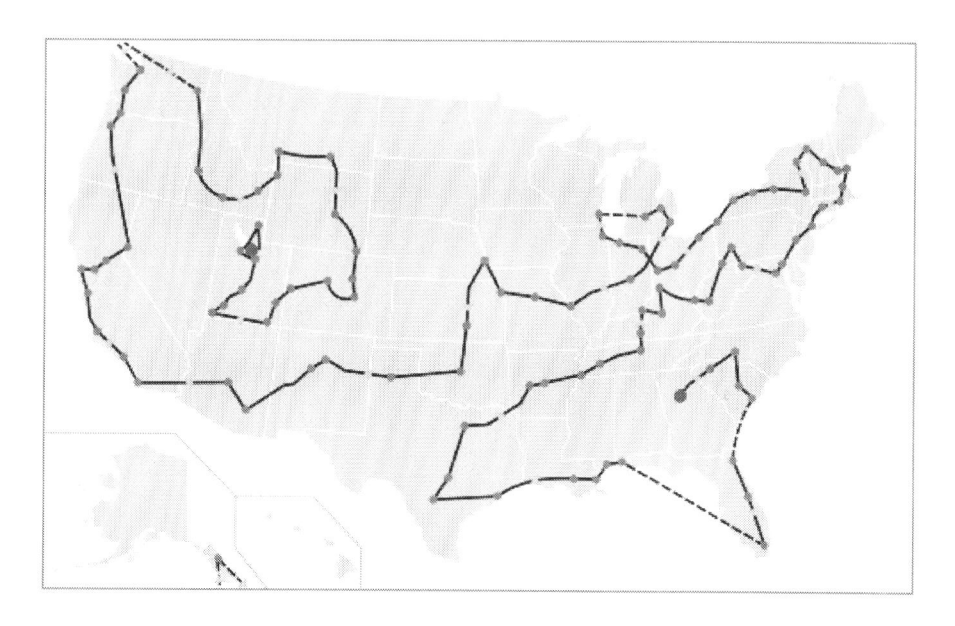

My question to you is: What do the Olympic Torch and I have in common? Yes, I know—we are both 'hot'! ☺ But what else? The answer is it took both of us 15,000 miles to cross the country ... one way!

This is My Odyssey.

After moving to Oregon, I came to a sickening realization. When we lived in Wichita Falls, Texas, we were halfway across the country and always drove back to the east coast to visit our family. But now in Oregon, we lived about as far from the east coast as you could get and still be in the lower 48 states. Driving back for short family visits would no longer be an option. It was fly ... or don't go.

For someone who does not like to fly, who really *dreads* flying, I was stuck. The only way we could visit our parents and our daughters in a reasonable amount of time would be to fly.

Did I say "does not like to fly"? Oh my, that is to *laugh!* I have a terrible fear, an irrational fear of, let's see ... how can I put this in a calm, mature, composed way ... of DYING VIOLENTLY!

I don't like the thought of being confined in a narrow metal tube so heavy with people and luggage that it defies logic to *ever* get off the ground in the first place. I don't want to know that I am 37,000 feet up in the air without a net!

Are you familiar with the Bridge of Sighs in Venice? Whenever I walk down the jet way to board a plane, I feel like I'm crossing that Bridge of Sighs. Condemned prisoners had to walk from the Doge's Palace across that bridge to the prison on the other side of the canal. Etched on the bridge are the words of Dante from his "Divine Comedy"—

"Lasciate ogne speranza, voi ch'entrate!" / "Abandon all hope, ye who enter here!"

That's what I do whenever I have to board a plane ... I abandon hope and sigh. I ... walk ... as ... slowly ... as ... possible ... before ... stepping ... into ... the ... plane.

There's always a pleasant, bright-eyed, bushy-tailed flight attendant greeting passengers at the doorway and I hear a cheery "Good Morning!" I nod and attempt to smile while looking at her face, trying to detect any sign of worry. Sighing, I trudge back to coach—head down, shoulders slumped—looking like I've just been convicted. TERRIFIED PASSENGER WALKING!

Once I'm on the plane and take my seat, I go through a ritual. After making sure that cool air from the vent spout above my head is wide open and pointed directly at my face, I inflate my travel pillow and position it behind my head. Then I jam earplugs into each ear and fasten my seatbelt.

As the plane taxies towards the end of the runway, I whip out a stick of gum and begin chewing it like some ravenous hotdog-eating contestant.

As we rush and roar down the runway, I grip the armrests of my seat as tightly as I can and pulling them upwards as the plane leaves the ground, I silently mouth: "Gedup, gedup, gedup!"

I feel that I contribute immeasurably in getting the plane off the ground, in gaining altitude and in assisting in keeping it in the air. No wonder I'm bushed after every flight ... all that heavy lifting, don'tchaknow!

So far however, I have never gotten a Standing Ovation from the other passengers ... but if they only knew!

John, in the seat next to me, is always there and always shows his appreciation by not snoring too loudly.

But back to my odyssey ....

My flying dilemma came up shortly after we arrived in Oregon in August. John wanted to attend the American College of Prosthodontics Conference in Washington, D.C. that October, less than two months away. Oh gads.

October arrived. We left Oregon a few days early and flew to Chicago, then on to Newark, New Jersey. We rented a car and visited with our parents in New Jersey before heading down to Washington, D.C.

In addition to the Prothodontics Conference, John and Betsy, who was also in D.C. for a few days, wanted to run a half-marathon in the Marine Corps Marathon being held that same October weekend. As mentioned, we were also going to visit Jennifer and Chris, then stationed at Seymour-Johnson Air Force Base, North Carolina, after the weekend. We would fly back to Portland from Raleigh.

However, while John was at the prosthodontics conference, I came up with a plan that I thought would be the answer to my prayers, something that would let me travel across the country without flying. Namely, to could go by train, on Amtrak.

Excitedly, I called Amtrak and got their time and price schedules for returning to Portland from Raleigh. There were no sleeper accommodations available but I could purchase a reserved seat on the Chicago to Portland leg. The entire trip would take five days and cost around $225.

After the weekend, I presented my proposal to John as we drove to North Carolina. Jennifer had just had an operation on her collarbone and I wanted to stay with her while she recuperated. Since John needed to get back to Portland to return to work, I explained that with an Amtrak ticket I would no longer worry and stew about flying and that I could return to Portland in about ten days, when Jennifer would be well on the mend.

John was, understandably, not pleased knowing that I would not be using my non-refundable, non-exchangeable $600 return plane ticket, but he knew that I really wanted to try my new travel plan and being a good husband, he agreed.

We enjoyed our visit with Chris and Jennifer. Then John flew back to Oregon, which took about eight hours. After getting back to our home in Lake Oswego that evening, he called to let me know that his flights had been smooth and uneventful.

As per my proposal, I stayed on with Jennifer until she was doing much better. Then it was time for my return to Oregon.

Wearing my navy SAS wedgie shoes, navy crew socks, lightweight jeans, a white collared polo top and my navy windbreaker, I was, yes ... quite the fashion plate and could have passed for your typical runway model! Jennifer and Chris drove me to Raleigh early on a Saturday morning and I boarded the Amtrak train bound for Washington, D.C., 286 miles to the north.

Besides my suitcase and purse, I carried a small tote bag with a sandwich Jennifer had insisted on making, a can of soda, granola bars and the current book I was reading.

I took a seat next to a window and at the next stop, only three miles down the track, other passengers boarded. A pleasant older woman sat next to me and we struck up a conversation. Unfortunately, the train was soon hemmed in by trees on either side of the tracks for miles ... and miles ... and miles. It was like being in a green tunnel.

As I looked over at this woman as we chatted, I kept seeing the wall of trees flash by through the windows on the far side of the train. It didn't take long before I had motion sickness.

The train made umpteen stops and took almost 6 ½ hours to get to Union Station in Washington, D.C. With a two-hour layover, I had to haul my suitcase, purse and tote bag with me everywhere I went.

Cramming everything inside a small ladies' room stall was particularly challenging as was straddling my suitcase while washing my hands at the sink, then dragging everything over to the paper towels while maneuvering around other women with their luggage, mothers with babies in strollers and crowds, crowds everywhere. I found a food court, ate my sandwich and took two Excedrin with my soda. I couldn't wait to board the over-night train to Chicago.

The Amtrak train from Washington, D.C. to Chicago, called the Capitol Limited, was a massive double-decker. As I boarded, a porter took my suitcase to stow in the baggage compartment. I then climbed up a narrow flight of stairs to rows of reserved seats for two on the upper level. My assigned, reserved seat was on the aisle, opposite the stairwell and across from a soda vending machine. An extremely obese man was already sitting in the window seat, next to my seat. I have no idea how he managed to climb the flight of stairs but there he was.

I squeezed down next to him as best I could and we exchanged 'hellos'. The hard plastic, molded bench seat had two shallow concave indentations to indicate where to 'park your bottom'. My travel partner literally oozed over into my seat, leaving me with little sitting space. There was no middle divider or pull-down armrest to separate us. How did I ever get paired with Jabba-the-Hutt?

The train filled up and as we began pulling out of Union Station, the train swayed from side-to-side until it got up to the proper speed. It gave me motion sickness again so I ate a second granola bar to give my stomach something to work on.

While Jabba worked a crossword puzzle, I got up and walked back to the domed car, thinking that if I could look out the windows on both sides as well as up into the sky, I would feel better. I didn't. Other passengers had brought their dinners to the domed car. The smell of their French fries and other greasy food made my stomach flip so I went back to my reserved seat and tried reading my book.

It got dark quickly but in conversation with Jabba, I learned that he was on a business trip, returning to Iowa. He said that he never flew and I wondered if that was because he would be required to pay for two airplane seats.

Other passengers kept plunking quarters in the vending machine across from me followed by a loud CLUNK! as the can of soda dropped down. The train stopped about every half hour to pick up and discharge passengers or to slip into a siding to let an express train zip by. The train lurched and the brakes screeched each time we stopped, making ear-piercing, grinding noises. With the constant stop and go and the constant swaying, I was miserable.

Around 10 p.m., a steward came along passing out cocktail napkins. After awhile, when the fresh shrimp and cocktail sauce never materialized, I discovered that the 4" square napkin was, in reality, my pillow!

I bent down and pried up my footrest, placed my $1/64^{th}$ inch pillow behind my head and tried to sleep. I couldn't.

An elderly man, sitting a few rows behind me with his wife, began to sing softly, "Oh Jesus ... yes, yes Jesus. You keep us in your care, we feel your love, we don't despair. Oh Jesus, wonderful Jesus ..."

I was wide awake but the singing had the opposite effect on Jabba who had fallen sound asleep next to me, snoring to beat the band! I raised my arm to give him a little *shove* when I remembered, hey, I can't do that. He's not John!

Between Jabba, the gospel singing, the constant CLUNKING of the vending machine, passengers talking and going up and down the stairs opposite me, the train's constant stops and starts, the swaying coach and the squealing brakes, I didn't sleep at all. And when I don't sleep, I get a headache and feel *really* sick.

Our arrival into Union Station in Chicago was delayed by two hours because of mechanical problems. What was to have been a relaxing 18-hour train ride became a 20-hour nightmare. I thought I would go out of my mind. I couldn't take it anymore. All I wanted to do was get off the train. I *had* to get off the train.

Looking at the train's schedule, I saw that we had stopped in Rockville, Cumberland, Harper's Ferry, Martinsburg, Connellsville, Pittsburgh, Alliance, Cleveland, Elyria, Sandusky, Toledo, Waterloo, Elkhart, South Bend and ... FINALLY ... Chicago, Illinois—14 stops in all. I think I could have walked to Chicago faster!

At the time, my youngest sister Marjie and her family lived in Glen Ellyn, a suburb of Chicago. I had made up my mind that I would get off the train, call Marjie and explain my situation. I thought that if I could go to her house and get a good night's sleep, I would fly back to Portland the next day.

We finally pulled into Chicago's Union Station around 11 a.m. Sunday morning and I was a zombie. Hoping to get a refund for the unused portion of my train fare, I turned in my Amtrak ticket, saying that train travel gave me motion sickness. Apologetically, the ticket agent could only give me a $30 credit. I didn't care ... I was off the train.

I called Marjie, but she and her family weren't home. Sobbing uncontrollably, I called John in Lake Oswego to let him know about my miserable failure regarding train travel. But he wasn't there either, so I left a message. Was there no one to listen to my pitiful, pathetic plight? While I waited to talk to them, I took two more Excedrin, had another granola bar and felt very sorry for myself.

Around 12:30 p.m., I was able to reach Marjie, who was immediately sympathetic. She invited me to come out to their home, spend the night and she said she would take me to the airport in the morning. I was tremendously relieved and felt like the weight of the world had been lifted off my shoulders.

When I told Marjie that I would take a cab from Union Station out to her house, she about choked. *"No,* don't do that!!" she exclaimed. "It'll cost an arm and a leg! Your best bet is to take the commuter train out to Glen Ellyn." ANOTHER TRAIN?? I shuddered at the thought but pulled myself together. I could do it. I just had to think positively. But first I had to walk four blocks to the Northwestern Train Station for the commuter line service.

So on a cold, overcast Sunday afternoon in late October, I set out on foot along the practically deserted streets of downtown Chicago, the wind whipping through me like a knife. My thin clothing, which I had now been wearing for 36 hours, provided zero protection from the cold, blustery autumn weather. Unfortunately, I exited Union Station on the wrong side street so instead of walking four blocks, I had to walk eight, which added to my despair. I was a pretty sorry picture as I plodded along, dragging my suitcase behind me, its' too small wheels catching on every sidewalk crack, causing it to tip over.

I finally reached the Northwestern Train Station and bought a ticket to Glen Ellyn. But because it was the weekend, the trains ran less frequently. I had to wait over an hour before the next train arrived.

I was cold and hungry and I didn't want to wait in the dark, dreary waiting room. I walked out a doorway and down a long hallway, dragging my suitcase behind me, until I came to a handsome broad marble staircase that must have led to corporate offices above.

Parking my suitcase on the floor, I plunked down on the wide stairs, hunched my jacket up around my neck and began chomping on another granola bar.

As I took my first bite, a security guard burst out from a side door, rushed up to me and barked, **"Hey lady! You can't sit there! Get off the stairs and move along ... NOW!"**

He thought I was a vagrant! All I needed was a shopping cart filled with my worldly possessions. I tried explaining that I was waiting for the train to Glen Ellyn but he wasn't interested. This was no place for the homeless—me!—to loiter. I wrapped up my partially eaten granola bar, stuffed it in my pocket, grabbed my suitcase and shuffled back to the bleak waiting room.

When the commuter train stopped at the Glen Ellyn train station, Marjie was waiting for me. She said I was as white as a sheet and shaking like a leaf. I don't remember that. All I remember is what a welcome sight she was!

She drove me to her home where she had prepared a lovely dinner. After a relaxing evening with Marjie's family, I slept like the proverbial log that night.

I woke up on Monday morning and called American Airlines. I was told that a one-way ticket to Portland that afternoon would cost $780. Did she say **$780**? I was floored! How ridiculous, I thought ... I am NOT going to pay that.

I called John and after discussing my options with Marjie and John, I decided that I would rent a car and drive the 2,120 miles back to Portland instead. Renting a car would cost far less than the plane ticket plus I had the time to drive back to Oregon.

Calling around, I found that I could rent a car from Budget at O'Hare Airport on Tuesday morning. As a one-way rental, it would be more expensive than normal but it was still less than $780.

Marjie and I then shopped for snacks, fruit and soda that I wanted to have with me for the long drive.

Betsy, who was working for Andersen Consulting and on assignment in Topeka, Kansas, had heard of my plight. She called me at Marjie's. Upon learning that I was going to drive back to Oregon, Betsy asked if I would head south first, to Topeka, for a visit. She said that she could take a day or two off from work and show me the area. I loved the idea!

Betsy also wanted me to meet an Andersen Consulting colleague of hers that she had been talking about. His name was Derek Wolf. John and I had been hearing how they jogged together on weekends, were out for dinner with other Andersen friends after work.

Hmmm ... I need to meet this fellow.

Borrowing an atlas from Marjie, she drove me to Budget Rent-A-Car at O'Hare early the next morning. We loaded up my rental car with my 'stuff' and, thanking Marjie profusely, I headed out of Chicago on I-80 West, towards Iowa. As I drove, it got colder and more and more cloudy.

Just beyond Des Moines as I exited onto I-35 South, it started to snow! Oh lovely. Here I was in a rental car, no snow shovel, no chains and no warm clothes. The snow came down fast and furious and started sticking and swirling on the interstate. Oh brother, I thought ... what have I gotten myself into?

Thankfully, I drove out of the snow and the sun came out, making the almost 600 miles to Topeka uneventful. Arriving at Betsy's apartment, we enjoyed a great 2-day visit—walking, talking, laughing, eating—just what the doctor ordered! Betsy showed me Topeka and drove me around the Menninger Clinic, the famous psychiatric facility. Fortunately, by that time, I no longer was in need of their services.

The second day of my visit, Betsy made reservations at Teller's, a restaurant in a former bank building in nearby Lawrence, Kansas, where Derek would be joining us.

Having heard so much about Derek, I felt like I knew him. And when I met him, I liked him immediately! He was everything Betsy had said he was and I was sure I saw sparks flying.

It was hard leaving Betsy the next morning but I still had a long trip ahead. My intention had been to head northwest back to I-80 in the direction of Portland. But when I had spoken with John the night before about meeting Derek, John informed me that a blizzard was raging in Wyoming. "DO NOT GET BACK ON I-80" he warned me, "HEAD SOUTH!"

I checked my atlas and the next morning, after saying goodbye to Bets, I continued south on I-35 to Oklahoma City where I picked up I-40 West. The sun was out, the roads were dry and I sailed along, gaining an hour when I crossed into New Mexico.

During a pit stop, I made reservations at the Best Western in Santa Rosa, New Mexico for the night. Because I had gained an hour, I ended up driving 730 miles that day! I wondered if perhaps I had missed my life's calling! *Breaker, breaker ... this is Merry Sherri, the White Top Mama, wishin' all you truckers out there a safe day. Ten-four!*

Arriving at the Best Western, an unaccompanied woman on a 'road trip', I was more than apprehensive. I had never checked into a motel by myself before. Ah, make that, I had never checked into a motel *ever*. John always did it for us.

Behind the registration counter was a corpulent, slimy guy sporting a pencil-thin mustache and a bolo tie. With an unctuous, lecherous grin, he purred, "Good evening".

No one else was in the lobby and he made me very uncomfortable. I tried to act as confident and self-assured as I could, as if I did this all the time.

Unfortunately, the registration counter was so high that I had to stand on my toes to fill out the information card, one hand holding the card, the other hand holding a pen.

"My, my," said God's-gift-to-women, "that's a lovely diamond ring you have there. Have you had it long?" Giving him a no-nonsense stare, I replied with an emphatic YES as he handed me a key. "Room 24, second floor." What a creep!

Driving over to the outdoor stairwell, I hauled my suitcase and food up to my room as quickly as I could. Once inside, I locked, bolted and chained the door and propped a chair under the doorknob for good measure.

Up bright and early the next day, I continued my way west, past Albuquerque, then past Flagstaff and Kingman, Arizona, before stopping in Needles, California. I gained another hour and had driven 646 miles.

Staying at the Needles Best Western, I called John once I settled in my room with a progress report … and a plea. It was a Saturday evening. I asked John if he would be willing to fly down to Oakland, California the next day, saying I would meet him at the airport and that way, we could drive back to Portland together on Monday. He always had Mondays off.

I was tired of driving by myself. I was tired of being responsible for the rental car. I was tired of not being familiar with the roads I had to travel and I was tired of trying to stay alert. In other words, I was tired of everything!

Being the good husband that he is, John agreed! Whew. I immediately plotted my route to the Oakland Airport, writing everything down in **BIG BOLD LETTERS** on a sheet of paper to refer to as I drove.

The next day, John flew down to Oakland while I drove 545 miles north to Oakland. We both arrived in the Baggage Claim area at the same time. How's that for timing!

We drove to a motel on Route 80 where we spent the night before driving the remaining 625 miles back to Portland. I was completely exhausted.

On the following map, I have charted my odyssey. Follow the dotted line from Raleigh, North Carolina to Washington, D.C., Chicago, Topeka, Santa Rosa, Needles, Oakland and Portland.

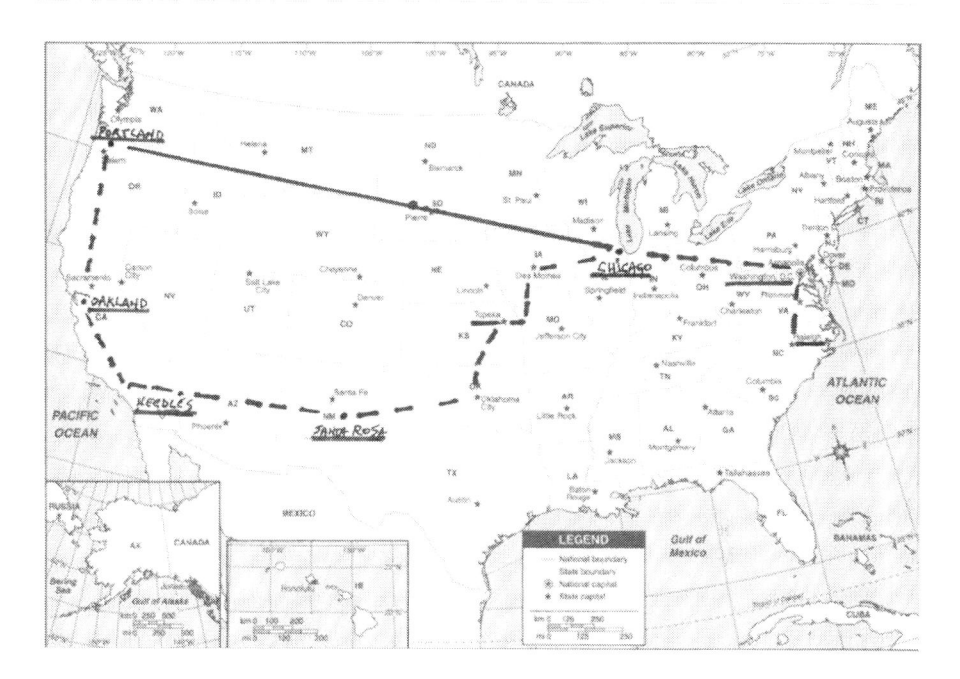

Once I got off the train in Chicago and after I rented the car, I drove 3,115 miles back to Portland. Did you ever? No, neither have I!

I probably should have just checked myself into the Menninger Clinic in Topeka when I had the chance.

Taking into consideration the forfeiture of my $600 plane ticket, the cost of the cross-country train fare minus the token $30 credit for getting off in Chicago, the cost of the commuter train to Marjie's, the expensive one-way car rental, gas, motels, meals, snacks, John's airline ticket to Oakland and miscellaneous expenses, my return trip to Oregon did *not* cost $780. Oh no, not even close.

I estimate my return trip cost $3,519, 687!

CR8O

Life in Oregon

After my odyssey, John and I settled in and eventually bought a home at 14360 Amberwood Circle in Lake Oswego. Over the next six years, we explored the Pacific Northwest.

Most picture postcards of Portland include beautiful Mount Hood in the background. Mount Hood is about fifty miles east of Portland and the highest mountain in Oregon. At 11,239' it is a prominent landmark.

Unfortunately, almost every time we had friends and family visit, Mt. Hood was nowhere to be seen because it was socked in, totally obscured by clouds or rain. I got so frustrated that I ended up calling it "Mount Hid". When it could be seen however, it was spectacular.

As you may know, rain is a frequent occurrence in the Pacific Northwest, often euphemistically referred to as 'liquid sunshine'. Weathermen sometimes got to report that we would have 'occasional sun breaks'. Every article of clothing that I bought came with its own hood ... even my bras.

On Easter Sundays, folks would get up early to attend Easter Rainrise Services and we all know the famous "Hallelujah Chorus" from Handel's "MESSIAH". In Oregon, the choir sings: "and He shall *rain* forever and ever."

Some of the most beautiful places in the Pacific Northwest are the Columbia River Gorge and Beacon Rock, the Old Columbia Highway with its many waterfalls and Washington Park with its Rose Test Gardens. Also of great interest are historically significant sites from the Lewis and Clark Expedition, Mount Saint Helens and its volcanic aftermath, Seattle and Mount Rainier, the Olympic Peninsula and Vancouver, British Columbia. Butchart Gardens on the island of Victoria, B.C. is spectacular as are Banff and Lake Louise in the breath-taking Canadian Rockies. We saw it all and I am so glad that we had the opportunity to live in that corner of our country.

Betsy and Derek, both still working for Andersen Consulting, were married in Kansas City, Missouri, in August 1997 and Betsy became a "Wolf".

A year later and with new jobs, they moved to California and were *only* a ten-hour, 625-mile drive from our home in Lake Oswego. We were thrilled to have them living close by ... practically next door!

Derek is a fine young man and one of the nicest fellows around! A business development manager with a software company, John and I were so pleased to have another special son-in-law in our family. As you see from this photo, he is tall, slim and trim. I just wish he would share a little of his 'tall, slim and trim' with his mother-in-law.

Betsy and Derek have given us two more wonderful grandchildren, Emmy and Drew, who will be 9 and 7 years old respectively when this book goes to press.

On one sightseeing trip, John and I exited Interstate 84 at Twin

Falls, Idaho and drove south for 24 miles to John's namesake town, Rogerson, Idaho … a hamlet of doublewides, a gas station and a post office. I always knew John was a 'stud' but apparently, he is also part 'spud'!

We went to the Tournament of Roses Parade in Pasadena one year, something I had wanted to do since childhood when I watched the parade on our small black and white Emerson television in freezing cold New Jersey on New Year's Day. It was fabulous.

Living in Lake Oswego, we met some nice folks—Lynn and Marty Preizler, Pat Logan, and our realtor Trudie Wilhelm. We became great friends. Lynn and Pat lived across the street from us and we three gals walked together all the time.

A couple of years later, Lynn and Marty moved back to Wisconsin. Pat and I continued our daily walking and one morning she told me about something that had happened a couple of days earlier.

As she apparently always did, Pat had taken her rings off before going to bed—her engagement and wedding rings, and her beloved grandmother's gold wedding band—and had set them down on top of her bedroom dresser.

The next morning she scooped them up and carried them downstairs to her kitchen. She put them in the overhead cupboard next to the sink while she washed up some pots and pans from the night before.

Once everything was cleaned up, Pat opened the cupboard to put on her rings and discovered that her grandmother's wedding band wasn't there. It wasn't in the cupboard or on the kitchen floor. She retraced her steps, searching high and low, but there was no gold wedding band anywhere. She was terribly upset, frustrated and mad because she had been very close to her grandparents and her grandmother's wedding band meant a great deal to her.

A couple of weeks later, Pat and her husband went on vacation and Pat asked if I would 'mind her cats' while they were away. While I took care of them, I tried to find the missing ring.

I checked under Pat's bedroom dresser with a flashlight, patted down the carpeted stairs, poking in every corner, and looked all around her hardwood floors. I thought it would be neat if my 'fresh eyes' could spot the ring and surprise her with it when she returned from their trip. Unfortunately, I never found it but Pat appreciated my effort.

Pat continued looking for her grandmother's ring whenever she cleaned and would from time-to-time mention how disappointed she was that it had never been found.

A couple of *years* later, after both John and I had moved to the Villages, Pat came for a week's visit. Like other proud Villagers, we loved showing her around our beautiful retirement community.

Before taking Pat back to the Orlando Airport for her return flight to Portland the following Saturday, I was the first one up that morning and was reading *The Daily Sun*, our Villages' newspaper. An article caught my attention.

A woman here in the Villages had lost a treasured keepsake. According to the article, this woman had prayed to St. Anthony, the Patron Saint of Lost Things, saying *"Tony! Tony!, turn around. Something's lost that can't be found."* The woman said she had recited the prayer three times in the location she had last seen the missing item and incredibly, not long after, she found it!

Remembering Pat's grandmother's ring, I got a large index card and wrote this prayer and the instructions down for Pat. Telling her about this woman's story, I told Pat to put the index card in her suitcase and when she got back to Oregon, to recite the prayer three times in her bedroom. Nothing ventured, nothing gained, I said.

The following Saturday afternoon, Pat phoned me from Oregon, saying that she had been cleaning her house that morning. (We had the three-hour time difference).

She said that when she had unpacked her suitcase six days earlier, she found the index card, stood by her bedroom dresser and did as the card instructed.

She then proceeded to tell me what had just happened.

The first floor of Pat's house had a half-bath built into the wall of the carpeted stairs, which went up to the bedrooms on the second floor. The half-bath had one of those sliding pocket doors.

Pat had been mopping her hardwood floor near that half-bath when she noticed something stuck under the open pocket door, in its track. She bent down to pick it up but the object was jammed. Pulling and moving it from side-to-side, she finally got it out. It was a black rubber washer.

Wondering if anything else might be stuck under the door in the track, Pat said she reached waaay in and felt something. With a little effort, she was able to wiggle it out and it was ... her grandmother's gold wedding band!

Pat said that she must have dropped the ring on the carpeted stairs going down to her kitchen that morning several years before. The carpet prevented the falling ring from making a sound.

With cats loving to bat things around, Pat figured her two cats had found the ring, played with it, batted it off the stairs down onto the hardwood floor, and kept batting it until ... oops, it slid under the pocket door into that track. Then frequent opening and closing of the pocket door had pushed the ring further back on the track each time.

Pat was ecstatic and I was thrilled for her. This story still gives me goosebumps and I bet it does you too.

John and I spent a day at Mount Rushmore in Rapid City, South Dakota during a road trip in 1998.

If you recall from my first book *Don't Set the Alarm!*, John and I had first visited Mount Rushmore in 1967. A dark-haired young woman, then 23, had apparently wanted to join the four distinguished Presidential heads:

Thirty-one years later, a more mature version of that same gal, no longer quite as young at 54, was seen at Mt. Rushmore again and, by golly, she was sitting in the same location.

But whoa ... what had happened to *her*? She must have made a terrible mistake one day. Instead of using shampoo to wash her hair, she must have grabbed a bottle of bleach by mistake ... the poor thing!

The Ham Sandwich

In 1998, Jennifer and Chris got orders to move from the Pentagon to Mountain Home Air Force Base in Idaho. They bought a home in Boise and were only 430 miles and one time zone away from Lake Oswego ... practically next door! We were thrilled to have both daughters and sons-in-law in adjacent states.

John worked four ten-hour days at the Tigard Dental Clinic, Tuesday through Friday (in addition to every night and weekends), BUT, technically, he had Mondays off. When we had a free Monday and it was convenient for Jennifer and Chris, we would take off early on a Saturday morning and drive the seven hours to Boise for a nice three-day visit.

One summer weekend, we scheduled just such a trip to visit our Boise kids. The Wednesday before, my regular grocery shopping day, I had bought snacks to take with us—fruit, soda—and two pre-packaged sandwiches, a ham sandwich with lettuce, cheese, mayo and tomato for John and a chicken salad sandwich for me, both on a hoagie roll and each in a clear, plastic container. The sandwiches were dated good through the following Monday.

Among the various things I was taking, I had packed a small, deep cardboard carton with some paperback books that I thought Jennifer might like to read. I put our sandwiches in the carton on top of the books so that they would come to room temperature as we drove and I put the carton behind my seat.

We left for Boise that Saturday morning but when lunchtime rolled around, John wasn't very hungry so we split my chicken salad sandwich and shared a soda.

Upon arriving at Jennifer and Chris' home, Jennifer emptied the carton of books and put the empty carton back in our van. I put John's sandwich, our extra sodas and fruit in Jennifer's refrigerator for our return trip on Monday. And as always, we had a great visit with Jennifer and Chris.

That Monday morning, as we loaded everything up in our van for our drive back to Lake Oswego, I again put John's sandwich in the now-empty book carton behind me.

After enjoying some delicious meals over the weekend, we grazed on nuts, granola bars and soda to keep us awake as we drove back home.

When we got back to Lake Oswego, we went through our usual routine of emptying the van. John carried our suitcases upstairs to our bedroom while I took our leftover soda cans, put them in our *garage* refrigerator and I put the small book carton on top of a chest of drawers next to that refrigerator.

The following weekend, that Saturday, John and I tackled some much-needed yard work. I mowed and edged our front yard while John weeded our back garden beds.

Getting thirsty, I grabbed a cold soda from our garage refrigerator and as I started to drink it, I noticed the small carton sitting on the top of the chest of drawers.

Aaah yes, the carton with the paperback books, I remembered. Suddenly an uneasy thought popped into my head. Lifting the carton flaps and peaking inside, there was the clear plastic container with the ham, lettuce, tomato, cheese and mayo sandwich sitting on the bottom of the carton! **YIKES!** I had forgotten all about it!

Not wanting to take the time to deal with the sandwich just then, I reached in, grabbed the plastic container with the sandwich, carried it into the house and put it on the second shelf in our kitchen refrigerator. I went back outside to finish up the front yard.

An hour or so later it was lunchtime and I was hungry ... time for another break.

Washing my hands at the kitchen sink, I looked out the window and saw John still hard at work in the back yard.

A yogurt for lunch sounded refreshing so I picked up a spoon and opened our kitchen refrigerator.

Reaching for a yogurt ... uh oh, wait ... where was the container with the ham sandwich that I had put on the second shelf? I looked high and low but it wasn't there. Where the *heck* was it?

I grabbed a yogurt, walked over to our kitchen trash can to throw the yogurt top away and stepping on the foot pedal to raise the trash can lid, I stopped in mid-motion.

There, inside the trashcan, was the clear plastic sandwich container, open and ... **EMPTY!**

I pawed through the garbage below it, but there was no sign of the sandwich anywhere. **OH ... MY ... GOSH.**

I began to panic as I mentally reviewed the history of that ham sandwich. I calculated that I had bought it eleven days earlier and that it had been sitting in the bottom of that cardboard carton out in our garage, **unrefrigerated** in the summer heat for the past six days!

I turned slowly and looked out the window again, into the backyard. John was still weeding.

What to do? What to do? How long does it take food poisoning to take effect? Should I tell John? The power of suggestion alone might make him sick.

I decided to wait. I would wait and see. If John started feeling sick, I'd tell him the story and rush him to the hospital.

Later that afternoon and getting up my courage, I asked John if he had eaten the ham sandwich. "Yup," he said brightly. "That and a Coke was my lunch." Oooookay, then.

You know what? John never got sick. He never even felt queasy or had an upset stomach. He was fine.

About week later, I made a new casserole for dinner. After cooking the noodles and browning ground beef and onions, I added tomato sauce, minced garlic and because the recipe called for it, cottage cheese.

John doesn't like cottage cheese but I didn't think he would notice with all the other ingredients. However, he could taste it and didn't like it at all!

I see. So a freshly-made casserole with fresh cottage cheese was not good, but an almost two-week-old, dried out, probably fuzzy ham sandwich with curdled mayo, moldy cheese, wilted lettuce and soggy tomatoes, was okay? Go figure!

John heard this story for the *very first time* several years ago when I was sharing it with friends.

As we sat there, holding our sides from laughing, John yelled out, "HEY, WAIT A MINUTE*!* *Now* I feel sick!"

The Lake Oswego Adult Community Chorus

When John and I lived in Lake Oswego, we received a monthly publication in the mail called "Hello, L.O", the township newsletter.

While reading the newsletter one October, I saw a notice about a chorus that met at the Lake Oswego Adult Community Center—the LOACC. Anyone over the age of fifty was invited to join (I was then fifty-three). They met on Tuesdays from 1-2:30 p.m., so I decided to go the following Tuesday to see what it was like.

The chorus met in the back room of the community center where there was a piano. Rosemary, the chorus director who looked to be in her mid-seventies, greeted me. Handing me a pencil, a nametag label and an information sheet to fill out, she said she would collect the information sheet at the end of the rehearsal.

Taking a folder of music, I sat down at far end of a single row of folding chairs next to a gal named Sue. I looked over at an old, battered upright piano off to my left. Sue told me that the elderly woman sitting on the piano bench with her arms folded and her eyes closed was Mary, the accompanist. She was taking a nap.

Six other women, also quite elderly, were already seated in the row of chairs to my left. None of them greeted me or even said hello so I just smiled and nodded in their direction.

I printed my first name on the nametag, stuck it on my jacket and began filling out the information sheet—Name/Address/Phone number/Email Address. That was followed by a series of questions:

Do you read music? Yes.
Do you play the piano? Yes.
Previous experience: Lots.
Would you like to sing a solo? Never!
Would you like to sing in a small ensemble? "Depends" (but not if I need them!)
What is your favorite style of music? Classical.
What are your three favorite songs? That was the only question that stumped me so I left it blank.

After filling out the sheet, I went back to 'Previous Experience' and after Lots, I added that I had been in church, school and community choirs for most of my life, that I had majored in music in college, had been the organist and choir director in a number of churches, directed and played the piano for the Air Force "Skylarks", etc. Why not toot my own horn? I thought. I have a pretty good résumé so I may as well list it.

When no one else showed up, Rosemary had us warm up singing "me, may, ma, mo, moo" and with that, another woman arrived. She sat down at the far end with the other six ladies and I overheard one of them say to her, "We have a new one." (meaning me) The group looked over at me in unison and I felt like a window display in Macy's Department store.

I hadn't sung in a number of years and the first song Rosemary had us sing was "The Autumn Leaves", in unison. It was high, at the upper limits of my vocal range and it has a lot of sustained words: The falling leeeeeaves ... Drift by my windoooooooow ... The autumn leeeeeaves ... Of red and goooooooold....

I was gasping for breath and the song was awful. The chorus screeched and warbled through "Autumn Leaves" twice. Rosemary seemed satisfied.

Next Rosemary had us sing "Row, row, row your boat", first all together and then as a round. Rosemary asked us to sing "Row, Row" as a round again but this time she wanted us to sing it with 'motions'.

She had us stand up and turn a little so that we could "pretend paddle" a canoe, first to one side, then the other. *Oh goody*, I thought. We sang through it twice with our "choreography".

Pleased with our efforts, Rosemary proudly announced that she was considering having the chorus sing this piece for the upcoming Christmas concert. *Huh?* To keep from bursting out laughing, I kept clearing my throat, trying to stifle myself.

After we sat back down, Rosemary announced that Tansy and Gladys had phoned her earlier in the day, explaining that they would not be able to make the rehearsal that afternoon. Lucky Tansy and Gladys, I thought.

The next unison song we butchered was "I'll Be Loving You ... Always". Everyone sang at full throttle in their individual favorite keys—all over the scale and all over the place—holding notes, sloppy entrances, not cutting off. "Very nice!" cheered Rosemary.

She then whipped out "Mr. Sandman" which was in parts—Yay!

But Mary, the pianist, only played the accompaniment. She kept hitting wrong notes, made all kinds of mistakes and no one could hear their individual part, but it didn't matter at that point. It was absolutely atrocious. "Excellent!" Rosemary exclaimed.

I got out my information sheet and erased everything that I had written under Previous Experience. I just wrote "Yes" and left it at that.

We then had a short break but stayed seated in our chairs. With that, another 'new one' arrived. Now there were two of us.

Next, Rosemary wanted everyone to introduce themselves, tell a little something about ourselves, where we were from, etc.

Almost everyone had lived in Lake Oswego for many, many ... many years. However, sitting two seats to my left was Martha. Martha had moved to Lake Oswego from Montana to live with her daughter.

Rosemary beamed and said, "Tell everyone how old you are, Martha."

Martha replied, "Well, in two and a half months, I will be 90!"

Whoa ... good for you, Martha! I hope I'm still singing when I'm 90!

We resumed singing with "Don't Sit Under the Apple Tree", again in unison. This was followed by a unison rendition of "White Christmas" for which there was no music, just the printed words.

When Rosemary turned around to get more songs from her carton of music, I got out my information sheet again, folded it up and as quickly as I could, I jammed it into my purse.

After "America the Beautiful" and "Let There Be Peace on Earth"—all in unison and all ragged—Rosemary asked how many of us would be able to sing for the LOACC Christmas concert on December 22nd.

All the ladies raised their hands and answered with a resounding 'Yes! Yes!' but I shook my head no. When asked, I explained that we were flying back to the east coast to spend the holidays with our family ... and we were.

"Well," Rosemary continued, "for the concert we'll do 'White Christmas', 'Row-Row-Row Your Boat' with motions, our imaginary paddles, 'Let There Be Peace on Earth' and 'Don't Sit Under the Apple Tree'".

With that, I piped up. "Uh, Rosemary? May I make a suggestion? Why not make it 'Don't Sit Under the Christmas Tree ... with anyone else but me'? or how about 'Don't Stand Under the Mistletoe ...with anyone else but me'?"

Rosemary stood there, shocked, seemingly stunned! Her jaw dropped and she looked at me in utter amazement, saying she was *thrilled* with my suggestion and thought I was just the *cleverest* thing.

All of the other chorus ladies chimed in, saying that they loved my idea, too, and that we *must* postpone our trip so that I could sing in the concert with them.

Aaaah, wasn't that nice? How sweet and kind of them.

I thought, I just might have to turn in my information sheet after all!

CR80

Alaska or Bust!

After going to Hawaii in 1991, I knew that I wanted to visit Alaska, too, since one item on my 'bucket list' was to visit all 50 states. Oregon was as close to Alaska as I was ever likely to live and I wanted to take advantage of our proximity.

Since I would never even consider going to Alaska by cruise ship, I sent away for maps and booklets to help me plan a comprehensive 10-day driving tour of the state, beginning and ending in Anchorage.

Going to Alaska in late June, the only direct flight from Portland to Anchorage was at 10 p.m. It was a four-hour flight and we gained an hour. It was still light as we drove to Portland's airport and the weather was clear and calm. I was actually feeling pretty 'not-so-bad.'

The flight was good and we landed in Anchorage just before 1 a.m., Alaska time. Because Anchorage gets about 21 hours of daylight in late June, it was just starting to get dark as we picked up our rental car and headed to Elmendorf Air Force Base where we had lodging.

We spent three days seeing Anchorage, first taking an initial trolley tour to give us an overview of the city. Besides the regular tourist attractions, I was flabbergasted when we passed a large lake and saw that just about every Alaskan residence had its own floatplane for getting around this huge state.

After the trolley tour, where we learned about Alaska's infamous mosquito population, we bought Cutter's Insect Repellent™ and headed off on a walk around the city center. We admired the gorgeous baskets of blue lobelia, white alyssum, yellow marigolds, white and purple petunias and red dahlias, each beautifully arranged and hanging on lampposts everywhere.

Driving around Anchorage, I began to note street names on the map I was holding and found them wonderfully descriptive: Northern Lights Boulevard, Moose Meadow Lane, Tundra Court, Bearpaw Street and Captain Cook Drive.

More street names brought to mind the rich heritage of Alaska's native cultures, whether Eskimo, Russian, Aleut or Athabascan: Nenana Point, Tobuk Circle, Knik Avenue, Kodiak Street, Muldoon Road—

Muldoon Road?? Sure 'n Begorah and for the love o' Mike! How did they ever come up with that one, d'ya think?

With Alaska's breath-taking scenery and awesome beauty, John had a field day taking hundreds and hundreds of photographs. You'll have to come over sometime for an evening of slides! What's that? You say you're busy every night for the next five years????

Leaving Anchorage, we drove north to Denali National Park but because of heavy cloud cover, we could not see Mount McKinley, the highest peak in North America at 20,320'. While disappointed, we saw a dog-mushing demonstration and took the Tundra Wildlife Tour before driving north to Fairbanks.

Once in Fairbanks, we took a riverboat cruise, toured the Gold Dredge #8 and panned for gold.

Heading south again, we finally got to see Mt. McKinley (more about that in the next chapter) before driving to Seward where we walked up to Exit Glacier and saw many bald eagles in Homer. We returned to Anchorage a week later for our return flight back to the lower 48.

Our plane was scheduled to depart at 1 a.m. and in preparation, my saliva started to dry up and my heart rate increased.

Around 10 p.m., we drove our car back to the rental agency, close to the airport. After getting our suitcases out of the trunk, John went inside the office to sign paperwork. I remained outside with our luggage, waiting for John and the shuttle to the airport.

The weather was clear and sunny. I could hear the roar of jet engines and could see planes taking off. Every time I watched a plane climb up into the bright blue sky, I imagined myself on it, gripping the armrests, chewing gum like mad, and muttering "gedup, gedup, gedup."

Standing there, I looked over towards a parking lot and noticed a three-story building just beyond. And that's when I made a *big* mistake.

The building's entire cinder-block side was painted a bright blue. In the middle of the field of blue was a sign painted in large yellow block letters.

ALASKA CREMATION CENTER.

While we had thoroughly enjoyed our Alaskan vacation, this was not a sign I needed to see before boarding a plane.

After reading it, I am sure I turned ashen, which, come to think of it, would be how I would look inside the cremation center.

All that was missing from the sign was my suggested company motto:

FOR THE VERY BEST IN BURIAL CARE, COME SEE US.
AFTER ALL,
YOU'VE "URN-ED" IT!

Mosquitoes

They weren't kidding. Mosquitoes in Alaska are BIG, RELENTLESS and EVERYWHERE. You know how Alaska likes to brag about being our largest state? Well, their mosquitoes have to be the biggest in *all* of America. They are SUPER-SIZED and could be classified as the 'State Bird'.

The mosquitoes aren't too annoying in the cities, but once you get out in the countryside, watch out! You might have five seconds before those blasted creatures detect your presence. They appear out of nowhere, then start circling, swarming and begin their harassment.

Driving around the state as we did, I saw folks constantly swatting themselves, their arms flailing and hands swishing the air as they attempted to fend off mosquitoes who think every day is Thanksgiving.

As recommended, we had bought Cutter's Insect Repellent™ and dutifully applied it daily to our face, neck, arms and any other exposed skin. The one surface I never considered was my rear end, but then, why would I?

We spent our first three days in and around Anchorage and the Cutters had proven effective.

On the fourth day, we headed out to Denali National Park, 239 miles north at milepost 239.

With all the driving we did, I was pleased to see that Alaska had portable toilets everywhere we went, in countless state parks and roadside viewing areas. They came in many shapes and sizes, from the cramped green vinyl "phone-booth size" to more permanent structures with shingled roofs on concrete foundations, some with flush toilets and running water. I used them all.

We drove just over 2,000 miles in our rental car during our ten-day vacation. With John making countless stops, taking over 1,000 photos on our trip, and figuring one bathroom visit every two stops, that's a lotta loos!

After leaving Anchorage and getting out into more rural countryside, my 'port-a-john' education was just beginning.

As you know, we did a lot of sight-seeing on our way up to

Fairbanks and as we headed south from Fairbanks, we noticed that the cloud cover hanging over the Alaska Range was beginning to lift.

We exited at milepost 147 at the Alaska Veterans Memorial, hoping against hope that we might get to see Mt. McKinley before leaving Alaska.

Entering the Ranger Station, we met military veterans who volunteered their time to run the small gift shop, answer tourists' questions and maintain the grounds.

We were directed to a grove of trees to see the memorial and its poignant statue—a helmeted GI looking through binoculars from his position atop a large boulder. A parka-hooded Eskimo is standing right behind him pointing towards the Alaska Range and Mt. McKinley.

Looking out in the same direction through a large, cleared area, we suddenly spotted the biggest mountain we had ever seen, massive Mt. McKinley at 20,320'. It towered over its neighboring peaks and was truly a magnificent sight.

A number of portable toilets with shingled roofs sat next to the parking lot—some of the nicest I had seen on our trip. I hesitate describing any portable toilet as "nice", but these were specifically designated for MEN and WOMEN. They were large, clean, light and airy. My ten-minutes between bathroom stops had expired so it was time to check out this latest facility.

Once inside, I had just bolted the door when I noticed that the toilet was sitting up on a concrete slab to accommodate the handicapped. Being vertically challenged, I couldn't reach the seat, which presented a definite personal problem.

When it comes to port-a-johns, I *never* sit down, ever, but assume the "hover" position instead. Picture Rodin's "The Thinker" *just* about to sit and looking rather tense. That was me.

I unwound a wad of toilet paper and put it in my right hand. Standing on my tiptoes for increased height, I backed up and put the soles of my feet up against the concrete slab, grabbed the handrail on the wall for support and leaned back as far as I could over the 'loo'.

As I was waiting for nature to take its course, I saw an enormous mosquito glide slowly past my knees, circle around and come back for another fly-by. I am sure its wingspan would have supported a wing walker. AND, the mosquito looked hungry.

Being in a rather precarious position, I felt trapped. I made an ineffectual swat at the mosquito and almost fell over!

I gripped the handrail tighter and kept batting at this intruder of my personal space, but the mosquito backed off only slightly, just beyond my reach, then flew in close again.

The mosquito continued drifting in circles around my knees while taunting—"Nah-nah-nah-nah NAH NAH! You ca-an't catch me!"

I momentarily let go of the handrail and tried swatting it with my other hand but that made me lose my balance again. YIKES!

The mosquito gave me a smirk and a big ole wink, as if she had just thought of something. I would swear that she waved at me as she floated up past my elbow and disappeared around to my backside.

There, of course, was my big white you-know-what hanging out in all its glory. NOOOOOOOOOOO!!!

To the mosquito it probably looked like Domino's had just delivered a large white pizza. At that point, I am *sure* I heard the mosquito smack her lips, snap open a napkin, tuck it under her chin and say Grace.

I went into a crazed frenzy. While trying to finish up my 'business', I began fanning my backside as rapidly as I could, to keep the mosquito from lighting.

Holding tightly to the handrail with my left hand, I fanned my backside with my right hand ... fan!fan!fan!fan!fan!fan!fan! Then, switching hands while still holding the TP, I fanned, fanned, fanned from the other side.

I was a spastic wreck with my efforts, trying to maintain my shaky balance while not wanting to be a target. No doubt with all my flailing away, I looked like a reeeeeally bad disco dancer.

Where was that mosquito and what was she doing back there anyway?

I finished up, grateful that I had escaped the mosquito's attacks. Whew, what a relief ... on two counts! I got myself back in order and got the heck out of there.

A few minutes later, back in our car as we resumed driving, a massive itchy area erupted on my rear and I began squirming to scratch it.

Geesh, that maddening mosquito had been successful after all. She was probably down in the holding tank of the portable toilet, chuckling and describing her lunch feast to her mosquito friends.

"I tell you, girls ... you should have seen that woman doing a herky-jerky 'Shake Your Groove Thing ... Shake Your Groove Thing, Yeah-Yeah!' It was a riot!"

Darn that blasted mosquito anyway. She not only "bugged-the-heck out of me", she was a real pain-in-the-butt!

☙❧

September 11, 2001 - 9/11

While John and I had enjoyed living in the Pacific Northwest, we had heard about a place in Florida called The Villages.

During a trip back east in late 2000 for Christmas, we visited The Villages and liked what we saw. Before we knew it, we had put a deposit down on a lot and were discussing which model home we wanted built on it sometime in the future. At the time, we had a year to decide.

In the spring of 2001, John decided that he would retire from Permanente Dental Associates the following spring, in 2002, but that I would move to the Villages before then.

We put our Amberwood home on the market and it sold the first day. Since the family who bought it wanted to be in our house by the end of May, John and I moved back to the same apartment complex in Lake Oswego where we had first lived six years earlier.

We rented a one-bedroom apartment and moved what furniture we needed into the apartment ourselves.

That was a job. Renting a Penske truck, the two of us carried a couch, a La-Z-Boy, tables and lamps, a card table and folding chairs, a bed-frame, box-spring and mattress, linens, food supplies, cooking utensils, plates, dishes ... what have you ... into the truck and then offloaded everything at the apartment. As I said earlier, military wives know moves! The rest of our household goods and furniture was put in storage by Allied Van Lines who would move it to The Villages.

In July 2001, John and I flew back to The Villages and spent a week ordering our home. We were told that our house would be finished and ready for occupancy by late October.

We flew back to Lake Oswego and life in the apartment hummed along. John continued working and I started planning for my move to The Villages in October.

On Tuesday, September 11, 2001, I was up at my usual 5:30 a.m. west coast time. I always turned on our television right away and watched the NBC affiliate station in Portland, KGW. Their newscaster, Brenda Braxton, was reporting the news and their morning meteorologist Dave Salesky gave the weather report.

About twenty minutes later, around 5:50 a.m., Brenda said there was breaking news out of New York City, that a plane had hit one of the World Trade Center towers. She said they were going to go *live*, directly to the TODAY show, which was already in progress.

And with that, Katie Couric and Matt Lauer appeared on my TV screen. (Because of the time difference, we saw the TODAY show at 7 a.m. Pacific time, via tape, when it was already 10 a.m. in New York City).

Katie and Matt were saying that it was perfectly clear morning in New York, yet a plane had flown into the north tower of the World Trade Center. How could that happen on such a clear, bright morning, they wondered.

It had actually happened four minutes earlier ... at 8:46 a.m. Eastern Time. The TV screen then showed a gaping, smoking hole near the top of the WTC north tower, where American Airlines Flight 11 had hit.

Katie thought it might have been a small, private plane that had had mechanical problems. Katie and Matt took a quick station break and came back on the air at 9 a.m. They continued discussing the plane, an apparent accident. The NBC television camera was showing the burning WTC north tower, when, at 9:03 a.m., they watched on their monitors and I watched on television as the second plane, United Airlines Flight 175, slammed into the south tower of the WTC and burst out the far side of the skyscraper in a giant fireball.

I remember Matt Lauer saying, "Did you see that? Did you ***SEE*** that?"

Our world changed in that instant. These were no accidents.

John got up at 6:15 a.m. that morning, 9:15 a.m. in New York. I immediately told him that two planes had hit the World Trade Center and both towers were on fire.

Jim Miklaszewski, known as Mik, was the chief Pentagon correspondent that morning. I remember watching his report and, as Google confirms, "Mik was reporting live for the TODAY show on September 11, 2001 when a plane hit the Pentagon." That happened at 9:37 a.m. I remember Jim saying something about construction work being done on the far side of the Pentagon, and perhaps some equipment or paint cans had exploded, but it was American Airlines Flight 77, crashing into the Pentagon.

Regular television broadcasting stopped and every station across the country was reporting the story. Soon thereafter, we learned what had actually happened—four planes had been hijacked.

The south tower of the WTC collapsed at 9:59 a.m. and United Airlines Flight 93 plummeted into a field near Shanksville, Pennsylvania at 10:03 a.m. The north tower of the WTC collapsed at 10:28 a.m. Television stations continued reporting the unfolding events around the clock, for the next four days ... without commercial breaks.

All planes in the air had to land immediately and no planes flew for the next week.

I was supposed to play golf that Tuesday afternoon but I canceled. I was glued to our television set for the rest of the day and the rest of the week, listening to Tom Brokaw fill us in as more details became known. Tremendously saddened, I felt on-edge, my nerves taut.

The next day, NBC aired footage of the Changing of the Guard at Buckingham Palace in London from earlier that morning. The Guards' band had played "The Star-Spangled Banner" in sympathy and in tribute to America, a touching gesture.

The final count: 2,976 innocent people were killed on 9/11 ... murdered. Our country was in shock. In an outpouring of grief, our hearts went out to all the families and friends of those who had died. Their stories were heart wrenching as they continued to hope that their loved ones had somehow survived the horror.

I had an email from my friend Cathy Wiles later that day which I printed out and saved. Titled "Oh what a horrific day!!", she had expressed the events of the day so well:

> "I know this is just the beginning of the tragedy that will unfold in the coming days. Think of all the innocent lives that have been crushed because of this. Imagine the terror felt by all those people in those planes as they were flown to their deaths—I JUST CAN'T IMAGINE IT!!!"

In early October 2001, one month later, John and I left Oregon to drive across the country to The Villages in Florida. Our new home was ready and waiting. All of our stored household goods and furniture would be delivered to our new house shortly after we arrived. John was going to help me settle in, then fly back to Portland to continue working until April 2002, when he would retire.

In our 3,000-mile drive across the country, *every* car, *every* house, *every* bridge, structure, business and building, *everyone* was flying or displaying the American flag. It was heart-warming to see our country pull together and unite like that, honoring and remembering all those who had died on the 11th of September. We will never forget … ever.

Coincidentally, I have just finished writing this chapter today, May 2, 2012, the one-year anniversary of Osama Bin Laden's death.

One year ago today, Osama Bin Laden was shot and killed by our courageous U.S. Navy Seals. R.I.H., Osama … Rot in Hell.

૱

♫ It's a "Schmall Vorld" After All! ♫

I began life in The Villages in late October 2001 and gradually got to know my way around. Other houses on our street had been built, so I met the few neighbors who had already moved in.

John flew back to The Villages for Christmas and New Year's, which was wonderful, since I had a 'honey-do' list a mile long!

In January 2002, after John returned to Oregon to finish up treatment on his patients, my college roommate Bunny and her husband Tom, came to visit. Living in Pennsylvania, they had driven to Florida for a winter getaway. We had a nice time catching up and I enjoyed showing them around my brand new retirement community.

On their last night, Tom treated the three of us to dinner at Katie Belle's, a restaurant designed and built to resemble an old time saloon and dance hall. We ate on the second floor, overlooking the entertainment and dance floor below.

At the time, Katie Belle's had a salad bar up on the second floor, too, so after being seated at our table we got in the salad-bar line. Having lived in The Villages for just three months, I didn't know anyone except a few neighbors.

Suddenly a gal came running up behind me and stopped. She looked at my college roommate and asked, "Are you Bunny?"

Surprised to be recognized, Bunny answered yes! With that, this gal excitedly looked back to her husband in the salad line and yelled, "Bob, it *IS* Bunny! It *IS* Bunny!"

I was dumbfounded. Here I was The Villages resident, but this gal knew Bunny? Incredible. I didn't know if she was a Villager or a visitor herself, but her husband came up and joined her in talking to Bunny, going over details about when they had last seen each other. I was clueless until Bunny explained how she knew them.

Bunny had a friend in Pennsylvania named Doris whose husband had his own band. The band played for parties and functions all over eastern Pennsylvania and western New Jersey. The gal who recognized Bunny had been the band's singer for many years. Bunny and Doris had gone to several of the band performances together and Bunny had met with this gal on those occasions.

For the record, this is how I remember meeting 'this gal' who is none other than ... Billie Thatcher! Yup, Billie Thatcher, one of the Villages' most talented singers and popular entertainers. In the years since this surprise encounter, Billie and John have sung together many times and have shared the stage in musicals, benefit shows and in fact, they have done entire shows together. Ain't that sump'um?

All Villages residents have moved here from someplace else, from near and far. Many of them have run into folks they knew back home or from somewhere in their past and they have interesting 'Schmall Vorld' stories. Well, we are no exception so here are two more.

When we were stationed at RAF Upper Heyford in England from 1983-1987, there was another Air Force family, the Curtons, that we had gotten to know. Ann and Eric are a little younger than we are and had younger children.

As the base psychologist, Eric worked in the hospital with John and Ann was a very loyal member of my Skylarks choir. We attended various hospital functions together. Ann has a great sense of humor and a terrific, contagious laugh. Her laugh *always* made me laugh!

Eric got an assignment to Lackland Air Force Base in San Antonio and the Curtons left England in 1985. Since our San Antonio home was available for rent at the time, the Curtons lived in our house for the year they were in Texas. In 1986, they were assigned to Colorado Springs, Colorado, and that is when we lost touch with them.

In September of 2009, John's headshot appeared in an ad in *The Daily Sun*, our Villages' newspaper, about an upcoming show that he was going to be in. That evening we got a phone call ... a "Blast from the Past!" It was none other than Eric and Ann! They had moved to The Villages from Colorado a few weeks earlier!

When they'd seen John's picture in the paper that morning they could NOT believe it. They said the dentist they had last seen some 23 ago had not aged at all.

We were thrilled! Ann has now been in some musicals with John and it has been great fun getting together with them again.

Okay ... here is my last "Schmall Vorld" story about someone who has just recently become a friend.

John has played and sung with The Villages' Swing Band since its inception ten years ago and they perform for several big dances throughout the year—among them, the Sweetheart Ball in February, the Senior Prom in the spring and the Masquerade Ball in late October.

At the dances, a table is always set up near the band for spouses or girlfriends of the band members to visit each other, share snacks and enjoy the music. When John is not singing, he often dances with the "band gals", know as Bandettes, who long to get out on the dance floor.

A little over a year ago, John danced with a new gal sitting at the table, Lois, who at the time was seeing one of the trombone players. As they jitterbugged and chatted, John asked Lois where she was from.

"New Jersey," Lois answered.

"Oh!" said John, "my wife is from New Jersey".

"Really?" Lois remarked. "Where did she live?"

John replied, "Northern New Jersey."

"OH!" Lois exclaimed. "I'm from northern New Jersey, too. What town?"

John mentioned that I had grown up in Ridgefield Park.

Lois cried out **"I did, TOO!** What was your wife's maiden name?"

When John said Sherri Probyn, Lois stood there, stunned. She exclaimed that **she** had had Mr. Probyn—*my father*—for a Sunday School teacher!! Holy Cow!! Pretty amazing, huh?

Lois Duncan had been Lois Houston back then, but we never knew each other. Lois is four years older than I am, which makes her *39* today! We were never in high school at the same time although we had several of the same teachers.

Living here in The Villages, you read and hear about 'Schmall Vorld' stories all the time, but I think my three are pretty darn neat!

CR₽O

'Mr. Villages' Moves to The Villages

As planned, in April 2002 I flew out to Portland, Oregon to attend John's farewell retirement party from Permanente Dental Associates. It was time for John to join me and live in The Villages.

Early the next day, a Thursday, with 'liquid sunshine' coming down, we rented a yellow Penske truck and started packing up everything in the apartment that didn't move (and probably a few things that did.). Getting a 'wee bit wet', we first hauled cartons out to the apartment's parking lot to the truck where John loaded them tightly to prevent any movement.

By 3 p.m., with all of our cartons stacked and tied off, we began packing the truck with bookcases, file cabinets, John's dresser, a couch, chairs, tables and other furniture items. We couldn't believe how much stuff we had crammed into that small apartment! I felt like a pack mule as we hustled the heavy items through the rain, trying to meet our inspection deadline.

By 4:30 p.m., I was tossing stuff out of our refrigerator so that I could clean it. I got the apartment inspected at 5:30 p.m. and after loading our mattress and box spring, John contacted Penske to let them know we were on our way to get a transporter.

By 7:15 p.m., we had a transporter connected to the back of our truck and John's sports car loaded and secured on top of it. The measurement from the front of the truck to the taillight on the transporter was 46 feet! We were our own convoy!

We managed to drive 200 miles that evening, stopping at a Best Western at 11 p.m. By 11:06 p.m., we were in bed and asleep! It had been a very loooooong day.

We were up at 5:30 a.m. the next morning and ready to hit the road. We spent a relaxing weekend with Betsy and Derek in northern California, which was just what we needed since we still had over 3,000 miles to go.

Continuing our trek on Monday morning, I was anxious to get a little driving experience under my belt so that I could spell John from time-to-time. (J ... O ... H ... N. Hmmm, yes ... that looks right.).

I took over on the longer, straight interstate stretches, away from heavy traffic. Since the steering wheel did not tilt and could not be adjusted, *it* and the top of my head were the same height.

As we drove from Bakersfield to Tehachapi in California and dropped down into the Mojave Desert heading towards Barstow, I decided that "Mojave" had to be the Indian word for "Land of Remote Air Force Base" as we passed Edwards Air Force Base. Whew … talk about flat and barren. Little did we know then that our oldest daughter Jennifer and her family would be stationed there, not once but twice!

We got to The Villages five days later, unpacked and John was ready to begin establishing his reputation as … "Mr. Villages"!

Call The Fire Department!!!

John quickly settled into life in the Villages. As soon as he completed another long "honey-do" list, he hit the ground running, joining various groups, clubs and activities. We both joined Village Voices and the Philharmonic Chorale. Additionally, John joined The Villages' Concert Band while I joined the New Horizons Band in 2005.

A year and a half later, over Labor Day weekend in September 2003, we noticed that our house and lanai needed cleaning. We had recently had an infestation of midges—"blind mosquitoes"—in our neighborhood. While they didn't bite, they were caked all over our gutters and soffits around our house as well as our front door and on our window casements.

John bought a power washer to do the job and that Saturday afternoon as he washed our house, I put a meatloaf together for our dinner that evening.

I left my kitchen a mess with my mixing bowl and utensils soaking in the kitchen sink and other items on my kitchen countertops while I responded to some emails I had received.

After John finished power washing the house, he started on our lanai. He moved all the patio furniture outside our screened cage into our side yard to wash it on the grass. That freed up the lanai floor for power washing. With all the new home construction in the area, dirt and grit had settled on absolutely everything on the lanai.

Before hauling the furniture out into our side yard, John took all the chair pads and doormats and threw them inside, into a heap on our living room floor to keep them dry. Pool noodles and a large foam lounge mat were also tossed on the living room floor. My messy living room now matched my messy kitchen. Dear Reader, you will see that there is a reason for this public confession!

While John was working on our lanai, I got a pop-up on my computer screen that there was no dial tone. (This was back when our computer worked on a dial-up system). Checking all the phones in the house, sure enough, we were without telephone service.

Walking out on the lanai with the power washer making an

incredible racket, I yelled, "**JOHN! ALL OF OUR PHONES ARE DEAD!!**"

Shutting down the power washer, we walked into the house through our sliding glass door into our living room but wait ... what was *this??* A siren-like noise was going off. It wasn't as deafening as our smoke alarms but it was a constant, high-pitched eeeeeeeeeeeeeeeeeeeee.

We went through the house wondering where in the world the sound was coming from. It seemed to be loudest in the kitchen and in particular, in the vicinity of our refrigerator. John brought in our six-foot stepladder and checked the smoke and carbon monoxide detectors around the house. They were not the culprits. Climbing up into our attic from our garage, John ruled out that the noise was coming from there.

eeeeeeeeeeeeeeeeeeeeeeeeeeeeeeeeeeeeeeeeeeeeeeeeeee

We looked everywhere. While the sound filled the air, we could not, for the life of us, determine where it was coming from. Was it somehow connected to the loss of our phones?

Using our cell phone, we called our neighbors up the street, Mary and Joe Doneth, to ask if their phones worked and to explain our strange circumstances. Their phones were fine and they could hear our eeeeeeeeeeeeeeeeeeeeee over the line. They said they would be down in a few minutes to try their luck at locating the mysterious sound.

eeeeeeeeeeeeeeeeeeeeeeeeeeeeeeeeeeeeeeeeeeeeeeeeeee

The noise went on and on and on.

Again using our cell phone, John called TheVillages Home Warranty office but it was closed for the holiday weekend. He then called the Neighborhood Watch folks who suggested that he call the Fire Department.

eeeeeeeeeeeeeeeeeeeeeeeeeeeeeeeeeeeeeeeeeeeeeeeeeee

Finding a *non-emergency* number for the Fire Department, John explained why he was calling and was told that someone would come to our house right away. Two minutes later a fire department SUV, a red siren bar across its roof, pulled up in front of our house. A fellow dressed in jeans, a baseball hat and carrying a walkie-talkie, got out of the vehicle and walked into our house through our open garage and into our kitchen.

eeeeeeeeeeeeeeeeeeeeeeeeeeeeeeeeeeeeeeeeeeeeeeeeeeee

John immediately informed the fellow that, as he had tried to explain over the phone, he did not feel this was an emergency but was hoping that the fire department had had experience with this same strange noise before and would be able to locate its source.

Unfortunately, the fellow looked puzzled as he heard our mysterious sound and he too was baffled. John showed him around the house, but like us, he did not know where the sound was coming from.

Back in the kitchen, the fellow got up on the ladder, took the cover off our smoke alarm and pulled out the 9-volt battery but ... eeeeeeeeeeeeeeeeeeeeeee ... that didn't stop the sound. With our 10' ceilings, the sound was just there ... in the air!

Mary and Joe arrived as did another neighbor who was curious to know why we had a fire department SUV parked in front of our house.

I was just beginning to wonder if anyone else cared to take a tour of our **messy** house when a HUGE RED FIRETRUCK came down our street and stopped right in front of our house!

Four firefighters jumped out of the truck in FULL gear—black suits with reflective neon bands on their arms and legs, bright yellow boots, helmets and oxygen tanks strapped on their backs! It looked like a scene from the movie *Backdraft!* A gal walked in with them but she was dressed in jeans, like the first fellow.

All of our neighbors were out on the street standing in front of our house, wondering what the heck was happening at the Rogersons! John considered passing out time-stamped tickets for the next tour.

Joe Doneth, our neighborhood computer guru who generously gives of his time to repair everyone's computer, suggested turning off ALL the power to the house. It was a great idea but ... eeeeeeeeeeeeeeeeeeeeeeeeee ... the sound continued. At least we now knew that whatever was making the sound was battery-operated.

With that, the casually dressed gal who had come in with the firemen began opening the drawers across from my refrigerator.

There, in the back of the second drawer down, was a gift Betsy and Derek had given us the year before ... a battery-operated grilling fork. About 14" long, the fork contained a digital thermometer to test the internal temperature of meat to determine if it was rare, medium or well-done.

The gal picked up the fork, turned it over and removing a panel on the back, she pried out 3 small AAA batteries. The eeeeeeeeeeeeeeee STOPPED!

The batteries were low on energy, which had triggered the warning sound to replace them. Even the fire department folks had never encountered anything like this.

It was obvious that news of the incident had spread throughout the fire station the next day when we dropped off a donation and a note of thanks.

So what, exactly, had happened? Why the loss of our phone service? Well, in power- washing the walls of our lanai, John had inadvertently gotten water into an outdoor phone outlet, which shorted out our phone lines. It was mere coincidence that it occurred just as the fork went off. Gadzooks!

It's a good thing our kids hadn't given us two additional grilling forks at the same time or the fire department might have been battling the dreaded ... Three Fork Alarm!

ೞ೩

Golf

I have played golf off and on, mostly off, for most of my adult life. For the record, I want you to know that I am not a bad golfer. Oh no, quite the contrary. I am an *atrocious* golfer. I passed "bad" years ago! The best part of my game is raking the sand traps. Sometimes my putting isn't too bad but other than that, my game is best described by two letters ... P and U.

John plays golf, too, and is much better than I am. He can hit the ball a country mile and when the rest of his game is 'on', he plays well.

For those of you who might not be familiar with golf, you always aim for par—3, 4 or 5 strokes per hole. One stroke *less* than par is called a birdie, which is great. But one stroke *over* par is called a bogey, not too bad. *Two* strokes over par is called a double-bogey, not so good. *Three* strokes over par is a triple-bogey, etc.

Knowing that, I once heard a golf commentator on TV rhapsodizing over the fact that Tiger Woods had played 136 consecutive holes of golf *WITHOUT A BOGEY*. Hey, BIG deal. So have I! ☺

John and I were out walking one Monday morning after having watched a major golf tournament on TV that weekend. Tiger Woods ... and this was before his personal scandal and downfall ... had lost by one stroke. I brought up golf as we walked.

"You know," I started, "I just don't get it. I don't understand why professional golfers don't play better. I mean ... take the top fifty professional golfers in the world. All they do is play golf ALL the time. It's their livelihood. They practice constantly. They can hit the ball to the right and make it curve to the left. They can hit the ball to the left and make it curve to the right. Why don't they hit the fairways all the time, every time? When they chip, they know how to make their ball spin backwards towards the hole. They practice putting from every angle and distance, endlessly. At the very least, why don't they all get birdies on every hole? What's their excuse? I just don't understand why they don't play better."

John looked over at me like I was an alien from outer space. "You have GOT to be kidding, right? Come on ... you've played golf. You know how hard it is. There are so many factors that go into playing well.

"First of all, every fairway and every green is different and each plays differently depending on local conditions that change constantly, as you play. Countless variations have to be taken into consideration ... dry, hard-packed fairways or wet, slow fairways. Hilly or flat? Are the fairways narrow and bordered by trees or wide open with lots of bunkers and sand traps?

"Take the wind. What direction is it blowing—with you or in your face? How much compensation do you need for a strong crosswind or a head wind? Your swing and your club choice all depends on the wind.

"Consider sand traps. Is the sand hard or soft, wet or dry? Do you have to compensate because your feet are above or below the ball as you address the ball? Can you even see the green and the pin location from the sand trap?

"Look at the rough. Is it cut closely or has it been allowed to grow higher, burying the ball? If you're going to chip the ball, how hard should you swing? Should you just chip it back out on the fairway or take a good swing to advance it towards the hole? Did you need to thread it between trees ... or over trees?

"Think about the greens. Are they surrounded with sand traps? Are the greens soft so you can get your ball to stop or back up easily? Or are they so hard the ball won't hold when it lands? Are the greens flat or undulating? Can you putt from below the hole without having to negotiate numerous plateaus, swells and valleys as the ball travels to the hole? How are you at banking a ball on a hill with the precise speed so that the ball will track the terrain in the precise arc to drop into that small 4" wide cup? How hard should you strike the ball when you are three feet away or fifty feet away from the hole so that the ball either goes in the cup or slightly beyond? You have to make infinitesimal adjustments in your muscles and transfer them to your putting stroke to get down in one or two strokes ... on green after green.

"Let's talk about swinging the club. What club will you need to compensate for wind conditions so that you get the proper loft with a tail wind or keep the ball low with a strong headwind? Has it rained recently so that the air is heavy with moisture? That affects the flight of the ball. When you swing, are you maintaining a good balanced stance, transferring weight properly? Do you keep your hands ahead of the club? Are you positioning the ball properly relative to your front or back foot? How high have you teed the ball for the club you have chosen? Do you use an inside-out or outside-in swing? Are you keeping your head down and letting it rotate with your follow-through.

"When do you decide to take a drop shot when you have an unplayable lie? Do you go for that low percentage 'Hail Mary' shot through the woods and over a stream while clearing a fifty-foot pine tree standing between you and the green? How do you maintain a precise swing arc so that the club strikes the ball and ground at exactly the same time?

"These are just a few of the factors that a professional golfer has to master. It takes unbelievable hand-eye coordination, concentration, and constant analysis to do what a professional golfer does. Practicing all the strokes in golf ... driving, fairway shots, chipping and putting ... can develop a consistent swing and a measure of confidence but no amount of practice can ever prepare you for *all* the conditions they face on any given day. This is why someone like Tiger Woods is so phenomenal. The consistency in his game makes his professional colleagues just shake their heads in amazement.

"And let's not forget a factor that few of us golfers ever experience ... the mental pressure of a make or break putt in front of thousands of spectators and millions of fans watching on TV. The putt that Tiger missed on the 18th hole in yesterday's final round would have put him in a tie for the lead if he had made it and there would have been a play-off.

"But no, he didn't make it. It cost him a possible victory and over $700,000 more in prize money. *$700,000!* **One putt!** I would say that is pressure. While not as physically demanding as football, basketball or soccer, golf is probably the most technically difficult sport I know. No amount of practice can prepare a professional golfer to play flawlessly **all** the time. It is just an impossibility."

He finally stopped talking. Other than the sound of our footsteps, there was complete silence.

"Well," I finally said, shaking my head, "I don't get it. I just don't understand why they don't play better."

What Happened To Yesterday?

As you know, my first book ended in 1974 when I was 30 years old. John and I had been married for eight years, we had two young daughters and a sheepdog named Barney. John had been in the Air Force for seven of those years and was about to start dental school.

So what happened? What happened to yesterday? Time must be speeding up because the older I get, the faster time seems to pass. Have you noticed that, too?

As I write this book today, it is 2012 and I am now 68 years old. John and I have been married for 46 years, our daughters are grown with families of their own and we have four grandchildren.

John, a board-certified prosthodontist, retired from the military in 1995 having served in the Air Force for 28 years. Where did those years go? He then worked for Permanente Dental Associates in Oregon for seven more years.

From the day John and I married in 1966 until I moved into our home in The Villages in 2001, I moved 20 times. Whew, how is that possible?

For those of you who remember my tent camping experiences in *Don't Set the Alarm!,* I retired from that a long time ago as well. Now we do 'motel camping' and 'Air Force lodging camping'. ☺

For the past twelve years—ever since moving to The Villages—John and I have driven out to California every summer. Our youngest daughter Betsy and her family live there and our oldest daughter Jennifer and her family (our Air Force family) move every two years and wherever they are, we visit them.

We travel on different highways and byways, sightsee along the way and visit old friends each year. These annual trips are my cruise equivalent and one of the best treats about being retired.

What follows in this chapter is a collection of brief anecdotes and what I hope will be amusing "Sherri-isms" that just don't fit in any of my other chapters. I've gathered them together under the subtitle that I call "Hodgepodge" which the dictionary defines as "a confused mixture". Hmmm ... confused though they may be, it's my book and I can do what I want, right?

HODGEPODGE

I joined the New Horizons Band in 2005, three weeks after it formed.

Jan Van Allen, a charter member of the band, and I play the 'orchestra bells' or glockenspiel, an instrument which resembles a xylophone. It is a horizontal keyboard of graduated metal bars mounted on a frame, which is played with mallets. We stand in the percussion section to the rear of the band.

When we lived in England, my Skylarks and John's Drills Brothers sang Leroy Anderson's "Sleigh Ride" one Christmas.

John had made a "horsewhip" by cutting two 18" long and 1"x4" boards, and hinging them together at one end. Holding the boards in front of you, you open the boards into a "V" shape, then vigorously slap them together. That makes a terrific whip-crackin' sound, which occurs at the end of "Sleigh Ride".

Our New Horizons band was going to perform "Sleigh Ride" several years ago and needed a whip sound so we donated the 'horsewhip' that John had made. Ward Green, our conductor for the piece, asked Jan to play the 'whip'.

The first time we rehearsed "Sleigh Ride", Jan put her mallets down and picked up the hinged-board 'horsewhip' as we approached the end of the piece. She held the boards right in front of her and at the exact point called for in the music, she smacked them together as *hard* as she could ... **CRACK!**

Ward was very pleased with the sound but he cautioned, "Watch out, Jan! You don't want to smash your thumbs between those boards!"

Without missing beat, Jan yelled back, "It's not my *thumbs* I'm worried about!!" The band howled and Ward turned beet-red!

Over the years, I've come up with various quips and a few things that have happened that I'd like to share with you:

****

"He did everything in moderation ... but when it came to boating, he went overboard."

****

Do you remember this charming little ditty?

> Lizzie Borden took an axe and gave her mother 40 whacks.
> When she saw what she had done, she gave her father 41.

If Lizzie Borden, a single woman, had lived in the south instead of Massachusetts, she would have been known as a Southern Belle. But after she whacked her parents, would she have been called a "Slay Belle"?

****

When our daughters were growing up, they would ask what we were having for dinner. When I said leftovers, they grumbled and groaned, so I decided to change my 'phraseology'.

The next time they asked what we were having for dinner, instead of saying leftovers, I told them we were having "The Week in Review."

****

Driving on I-15 in California one summer, and heading towards Las Vegas, we passed a billboard. In big letters, it said:

LAS VEGAS
The Seven Deadly Sins. One Convenient Location!

****

John took up clogging shortly after he joined me in The Villages. After completing a clogging class to learn the basics, he became a member of the Clog-Hoppers dance troupe.

He wanted me to learn clogging and join him, but I didn't want to. My idea of clogging is spreading a thick slab of cream cheese on a toasted honey wheat bagel.

****

I discovered that Florida has four types of rain: light rain, moderate showers, torrential rain and … carwash!

****

His opera record collection was so old and went *so* far back ...
HOW FAR BACK DID IT GO?
It went so far back that he had a recording of "Madame Caterpillar".

****

When we were first married, my mother told me about something she had read. If you want to remember something, write a note and put it on the floor where you'll see it. Consequently, John and I have done that our entire married lives. We put a note on the floor to remind us of something or a card on the floor to be mailed—anything we want to be sure to do, to remember. It was a great suggestion and you know what? It works!

****

My mother, Janice Probyn, and my sister Barbara moved to The Villages from New Jersey in 2006. There is a photograph of my mother in *Don't Set The Alarm!* taken when she was 25 years old. Now she is 92! She doesn't look it, does she?

Mother's Day, May 13, 2012.

****

Talk about being over-educated ... John has a B.A. from Rutgers University; a B.S. from Penn State; an M.M. from the University of Wisconsin; a D.D.M. from Fairleigh Dickinson University's School of Dentistry; and a post-doctoral M.S. in Biomedical Sciences from the University of Texas.

Okay. So ... do you know why John went into meteorology? Oh boy ... here it comes ... wait for it ... *because he has so many degrees!*

****

Did you know that after World War II, there was only *one* kind of grape that would grow in Germany?

Oh really? What kind of grape was it???

The only kind of grape that would grow in Germany after World War II was ... Concord!!

****

In March of 2011, Jennifer and our two oldest grandchildren, Allison and Steven, came to visit during their school spring break.

Both grandchildren had read all the Harry Potter books so we went to Universal Studios in Orlando one day to the Wizarding World of Harry Potter.

The place was mobbed and waiting times for every ride and attraction were at least an hour. Everyone wanted get on line to tour Hogwarts Castle first and take the "Harry Potter and the Forbidden Journey" ride but not me. I wasn't interested in volunteering for motion sickness.

Having read the first two Harry Potter books myself, I wanted to go to Ollivander's Wand Shop. Knowing Allison and Steven both wanted to buy a wand, I told John that I would find out how much they cost so that later, when they visited Ollivander's, we would treat them to the wand of their choice.

Additionally, our neighbor Rose had asked me to buy a wand for her granddaughter, whatever the cost.

So while Jennifer, John and the kids got on the long line for Hogwarts Castle, I got on the long line for Ollivander's.

Almost an hour later, I finally stepped into Ollivander's Wand Shop and along with a number of families, watched the wand keeper put on a wand demonstration that was cute, clever and entertaining.

From there we were directed into the jam-packed gift shop next door where thousands of boxed wands were stacked floor-to-ceiling. The wands, in different shapes, sizes and colors, were named for many characters in the Harry Potter books. Asking a salesgirl, I learned that every wand in the shop cost $29.99. Tourists were scooping them up by the armful.

I picked out a wand for Rose's granddaughter, one I hoped she would like, and then I stood in another long line to buy it. I got an inkling of what it must feel like to be a sardine!

While I stood there clutching the wand box, a couple who looked like they might also be grandparents entered the store and politely squeezed past me. As they did so, the woman stopped, looked at me and said, "Are you buying a wand?"

I nodded, "Yes, I am."

She frowned a little and then asked, "Does it *do* anything?"

I thought for a moment and then said, "Well, yes. It makes $30 disappear!"

And now, before I sign off, my final chapter……

ॐ

His Kind of Girl

In the spring of 2010, John was asked by our Villages Entertainment Office if he would like to have his own show in our Church On The Square that October. While concerned about all the preparation it would require, he felt honored to have been asked and accepted the invitation.

John felt that for his show to be a success, it should have enough variety to hold the audience's attention for the entire 90 minute performance so that's just what he provided. Besides singing, he did some comedy, played the trombone, the baritone horn, the violin and even did a highly energetic clogging number on a 4x6' sheet of plywood. Is there *nothing* that man can't do??

Because he was going to do a variety of things, John titled his show "Everything BUT the Kitchen Sink!"

I don't know how he did it but our friend Gerry Sherman was able to get John *into* a kitchen sink. Thanks, Gerry!

I was touched when John dedicated a song to me in his show. Written by Leslie Briscusse, he sang "My Kind of Girl". Do you know it?

She walks, like an angel walks,
She talks, like an angel talks,
And her hair, has a kind of curl,
To my mind, she's my kind of girl,

She's wise, like an angel's wise
With eyes, like an angel's eyes,
And a smile, like a kind of pearl,
To my mind, she's my kind of girl.

*Pretty little face, that face just
knocks me off of my feet,
Pretty little feet, she's really
sweet enough to eat...*

*She looks, like an angel looks,
She cooks like an angel cooks,
And my mind's in a kind of whirl...
To my mind, <u>she's my kind of girl!</u>*

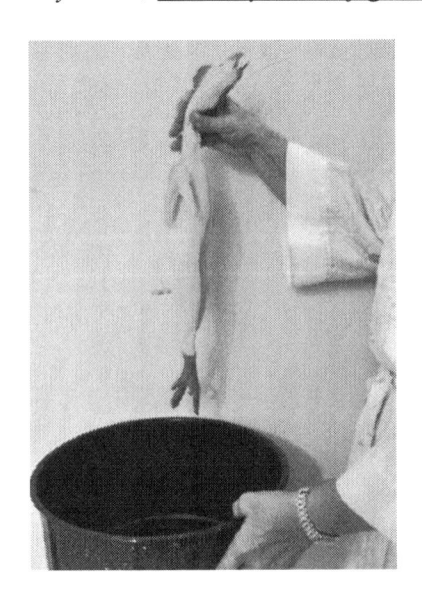

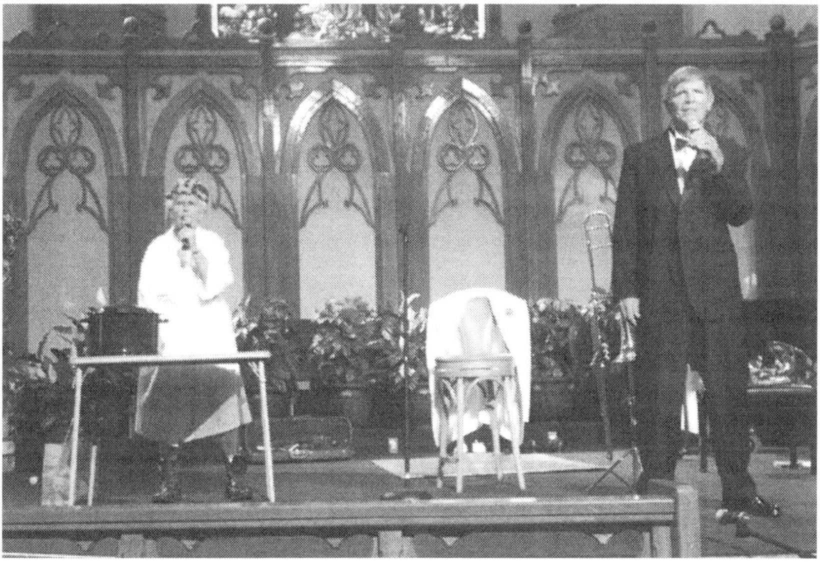

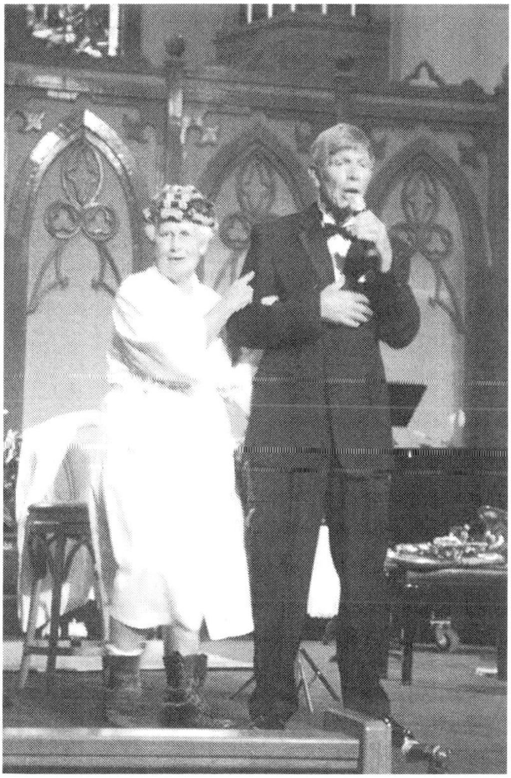

So that's it, folks ... the first 68 years of my life.

I used to have a 'bucket list' before that became a popular expression. When I was growing up, there were three things I really wanted to do:

1. Go to Hawaii,
2. Visit all 50 states, and
3. Attend the Tournament of Roses Parade in Pasadena, California. I have been able to check off all three and was thrilled with each of those experiences.

Do you have a 'bucket list'? If you do and are able, make your list come true. As Shakespeare himself might have said:

> "Doest thy 'bucket list' whilst thou may.
> Thou wilt never regret it!"

As I got older, I discovered something else I wanted to add to my bucket list ... to write a book and tell my stories. Now I have and I hope they have made you smile and laugh.

Thank you so much for walking down Memory Lane with me. I hope you have enjoyed the walk as much as I have in sharing it with you.

❧ Acknowledgments ☙

Thank you to our friend Geri Beck for suggesting *Living With the Late John Rogerson* as a book title years ago. It could not be more appropriate, Geri!

I want to thank our friend and neighbor Joe Doneth for all the photographs he took during John's "Everything But the Kitchen Sink" show in October 2010. If it hadn't been for you, Joe, I wouldn't be able to show my readers just how stylish and fetching I looked that evening!

Gerry Sherman, thank you for putting our slides in the proper format and for enhancing our Barney pictures so that I could include them in this book. Your willingness to help and your skilled assistance is greatly appreciated.

I want to thank our daughters Jennifer and Betsy for emailing various photographs they took when they were in their teens. Your pictures have added so much to my stories, girls. And Bets, thank you for assisting with the book's cover, particularly the curved lettering. That was a big help!

Mary Lois Sanders, thank you for your invaluable expertise in editing and formatting both of my books. It has been a real pleasure working with you. If any of you ever need a book edited or formatted, call Mary Lois!

The folks I mention by name in certain chapters of this book are included because they are part of that particular story. I wish I could acknowledge all of our friends and neighbors here in Florida and folks we have known for many, many years. But I was afraid that I might omit someone and I sure as heck didn't want to do that!

Finally, I want to thank the subject of this book's title ... *the one, the only* ... John Rogerson for being my first editor, for reviewing each chapter and giving me helpful advice, artistic assistance, and suggestions every step of the way. I couldn't have done it without you, John. Thank you for your love, support and encouragement in allowing me to pursue and complete a long-standing goal ... to write books about us and all the funny, crazy, silly, special, whacky, memorable, incredible adventures we have shared going down Life's Highway together.

☙❧

Other books by Sherri Rogerson

Order from any on-line bookstore

ISBN-10: 1456403192 // ISBN-13: 978-1456403195

Don't Set The Alarm!

- A Memoir -

By Sherri Rogerson

Made in the USA
Charleston, SC
25 September 2012